Amina Chatwin

You've Got Me Thinking

The Autobiography of Amina Daphne Chatwin
1927 - 2016

Published by
Reardon Publishing
PO Box 919, Cheltenham GL50 9AN

Amina in her garden

Copyright 2020
ISBN: 9781901037722

The autobiography of Amina Daphne Chatwin
1927 - 2016

With additional notes by the Editor
Julian André Rawes

Book and Cover Design by
Nicholas Reardon

Introduction

Amina lived in the centre of Cheltenham all her life and it was in about 2010 that she informed me that she had started to record her early years as it might be of interest to people, especially as the character of the town had changed so much. Gone were most of the local shops, tradesmen and their families, gone were the ladies and gentlemen who had inhabited the large houses, people from the military and administrators who had chosen to retire to Cheltenham from across the empire; she observed these social and cultural changes with disquiet.

Amina had finally finished her major publication *History of Iron Working in Britain,* a project that she had worked on for many years (yet to be published). And now turned her attention to her own life, which included her childhood in the 1930's and early 40's, her many interests such as dancing, puppetry, art, wood carving, architecture, dress-making, history, entertaining, early Christian art, iron-working, travels to Europe and America. She was a great observer and her memoirs are recorded with sincerity and openness, in which there is much sadness. Her book takes us up to her last trips to Italy in 2003-2004 and then ends abruptly. It is not known whether she intended to continue, her eyesight was failing through macular degeneration and she could no longer read and write without a powerful magnifying glass, a fact that greatly frustrated her. I offered to help her and by the time of her death we were part way through checking her final typescript copy. It was not an easy affair as Amina had very little patience.

After her death from a fall and hospital acquired pneumonia, I made myself a promise to publish this autobiography. The headings are almost entirely her own but the Appendix, and choice of photographs are mine.

I felt it necessary to add something about Amina's life during the twelve to fourteen years from her last entry up to 2016. Her travelling, especially when she had to give up her car, gradually diminished. She had also developed a heart condition and in later years often complained of lack of energy and being out of breath. She had little sign of arthritis and was a familiar figure around town until the end. She continued to put on her dinner parties until even these proved too much for her, the food was always superb and beautifully presented.

The dinner party

Amina had written books, articles and given talks for over 50 years, starting in 1960 on an article on ballet. It is possible to list only a few of them: a work on ballet that appeared 1961 in the Ballet Annual; *Don't Fence me In*, an article on Cheltenham ironwork, 1977; *Antique and Ornamental Ironwork*, Period Home 1985, Vol. 6, No,3 & 4; *Cheltenham's Ornamental Ironwork*, published in 1985, *Into the New Iron Age* in 1995; *Some Gloucestershire Ironmasters*, Journal of Historical Metallurgy Society, 1977; *Cheltenham and the Men in their Flying Machines;* a number of articles in the journal of the Cheltenham Local History Society; *Looking into Europe*, current Ironworking practises in Europe, 1998. And there is a surviving leaflet, which suggests that while still living in Wellington Street, Amina felt knowledgeable enough to give three talks, entitled *Early Christian, Byzantine and Medieval Art, The Italian, French, Renaissance Art and The Impressionists.*

Amina took a keen interest in Christianity and was an expert on early Christian art and custom and how it had formed. In later life, although an agnostic, she had joined the community at Christ church, her local parish church and in 2000, she helped to organise the Christ church Cheltenham Project 2000+. She went to bible study and talks and became part of the community. Amina seriously tried to have faith and to be a Christian, she was presumably spiritual but was intensely analytical and this need for proof made her critical of the Bible.

She could not accept that the Bible had all the answers without any backup from other sources or observations and could not simply rely on having faith in something. I remember an occasion when she had given a well-researched talk on early Christian art in which she stated that much of the early iconographic tradition of Christianity was derived from paganism. This connection with paganism had not gone down well with some members in the audience and she was asked not to speak on the subject again. She nevertheless found her visits to the church of great comfort.

Amina was accomplished in wood carving, as her puppets illustrate, and dress making; she also dabbled in painting and jewellery making. Her puppets have been donated to the National Puppetry Archive at Bridgnorth.

A self portrait

It is now clear that Amina had become a hoarder and her house was crammed with books, papers, clothes, slides, puppets, art, paintings, dress and craft making materials. She was fiercely independent and though her mind and interests were as sharp as ever, she still bought books and took an interest in international affairs but was losing the ability to sift through the mass of paperwork with which she had surrounded herself.

I dedicate my work on this book to Amina Chatwin whom I loved and admired, she will always be looked upon with affection.

Julian Rawes

A Childhood in Cheltenham.

In 2007 the architect who did such a good job on the rehabilitation of Christ Church, Malvern Road, said to me "I suppose you live in a Regency House" - well, I suppose I did - a coach house built in that period, but it was hardly what he had in mind. However, I had been born in a typical Regency terrace house.

The 1930s must have been one of the most uncomfortable periods in which to live in such a house. I was born in a house called St. Albans, in Wellington Street near the Town Hall in 1927. It had been named after the Duchess of that name, whose parents were of fairly humble origins and had lived in the nearby Cambray area. The Duchess was an actress Harriet Mellon, in the heyday of the Regency period and married Mr Thomas Coutts of the banking family, then after his death, as a very rich woman, married the Duke of St Albans.

Walter Vincent Chatwin, Amina's Father

My father was left £1000 by his aunt Amina (hence my name) and with it he bought the house shortly before I was born. The ground floor had probably once been two rooms with large wooden doors between them, an arrangement much used in Regency terrace houses. Down the side there was a long rather grand hallway, with an ornate plaster moulded ceiling, leading to a small toilet at the end. There was a fireplace at each end of the ground floor room and beside each a black rondel, inlaid, I think, with mother of pearl, and a handle to turn to ring a bell in the basement to call servants.

From the hall there was a tall flight of stairs leading to a shorter flight which led to three rooms on the first floor, two at the front and one at the back, above which were two small rooms.

When we began to live there the ground floor was given over to make a dancing school for my mother; we lived on the first floor, living room at the back and main bedroom and kitchen at the front. I should think all the rooms were about the same size, possibly the one at the back a little larger than the others.

Phyllis Elston, Amina's Mother

The only heating was a fire in the living room. There were gas fires in the bedrooms but these were never used unless someone was ill. In cold weather the house was extremely cold and talking to contemporaries recently we all clearly remembered the frost fronds of ice that used to form inside the window panes of our homes. The idea that one day we should live in houses heated by central heating was quite incomprehensible. Later the open fire in the living room was replaced by a stove type fire with doors at the front, which gave a better heat, instead of letting it all go up the chimney.

Looking back, I begin to ask myself where did we wash? I remember as a small child being bathed in front of the fire in the living room. At some point before World War II started, my father, who was a quantity surveyor and had been trained as an architect, built a bathroom on a flat roof at the top of the first flight of stairs, when a door replaced the original window. I can only think that before this we all washed at the sink in the kitchen.

Amina Daphne Chatwin

8

Presumably up to Edwardian times the people who lived in such houses had been waited on by servants who occupied the "servants quarters" in the basement, where there was a large pine dresser in the kitchen and a smaller one in the scullery. There would have been wash stands in the bedrooms each holding a large round china basin and a ewer (jug). I suppose the servants would have brought up hot water for washing. We did not realise it but by our time the servants had disappeared and the central heating had not yet arrived.

Amina Chatwin

When I was a baby I was for a time looked after by a Nurse Stenhouse. She must have been a rather odd character because one day she decided that she must go to London. With admirable care for her charge, and having no one to leave me with, she set off to walk to London pushing me in my pram. She wrote a note to my parents which was not discovered until late afternoon, probably when my father returned from work. At all events he set off in his car to find us and caught up with us at Northleach, so we had travelled quite a distance. I do not think that she remained long in our employ after this episode.

We took our holidays in Croyde Bay in north Devonshire. My father would drive us down and collect us at the end of the holiday. We stayed in the village where a stream ran down the side of the road. It must have made a tinkling noise because on returning home and lying in my bed at night, I missed it.

In the early years I was a small child usually in the charge of my grandmother. I am reputed to have gone into Mr Webbers at the village shop and asked for an ice cream cornet "but not too large". This was because the previous time the ice cream had fallen off onto the floor! Croyde was not far from Barnstaple where a local firm made pottery decorated with simple paintings and improving verses.

Amina Chatwin

For years we had a large jug bearing the verse:-

Do the work that's nearest
Though it's dull at whiles
Helping when you meet them
Lame dogs over stiles

Sometimes three or four young ladies from my mother's dancing school would accompany us. One year beach pyjamas became all the rage and some of the girls took the village by storm and were photographed by the local press.

On at least one occasion Ewart Norris was one of the party, a former beau of my mother's, who had been an aviator in the first world war and later worked in Africa looking after the Blue Posts Hotel, perhaps it was in Kenya. One day driving me in an open car, on a later holiday, he taught me a rather disreputable small verse:

There was a little sparrow
Flew all the way from Spain.
When half way on his journey
He met a great big hawk
Who plucked out all his feathers
And said "Walk you bugger walk."

They must have had a lot of fun, and an old photograph shows a rather sozzled looking Ewart being helped over a stile by half a dozen people. My mother must have regarded the beach as another form of stage and there are lots of photographs, over the years, of dancing and exhibition lifts.

Mostly I remember walking down through the sand dunes and looking for wild strawberries on the way to the beach. Yellow flowers were also common on the way covered with stripy yellow caterpillars. On one occasion when my grandmother and I were paddling, a large wave threw us off our feet, but we were righted again and suffered no harm. More than once we took our holidays in Highcliff, not far from Bournemouth; my father had a friend who had a "beach hut" there and every spring they went and put it up together.

Frances Day, Dorothy Blower, Celia Wilmore with Phyllis Chatwin sitting,

taken while at Croyde

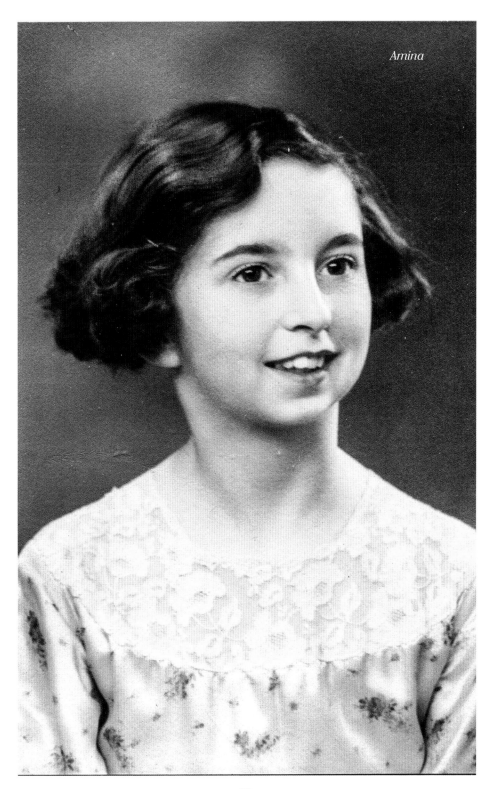

Amina

Amina at riding school

It was the way of coastal holidays then, the shore was littered with wooden huts of all shapes and sizes and I suppose one stayed in a bed and breakfast and spent the day living in the hut and sitting in front of it or on the sands.

In later years we went for holidays to Berrow, near Burnham on Sea, and my mother and I learnt to ride at a local riding school, riding most mornings along the great expanse of foreshore.

Back in Cheltenham I would go to Parrys and it was in their indoor riding school in an old chapel that I learnt to jump. Today it has been replaced by the Regent Shopping Arcade.

My grandparents (my mother's parents) had a small shop facing onto the street at 55 Winchcombe Street, near the Pittville Gates. Inside, a corridor led to living quarters and on the right there was a counter.

I suppose it was more of a workshop than a shop. He was a civil and military boot maker and used to make beautiful hunting boots with pinky coloured tops. My grandfather sat on a low wooden chair making shoes and boots. Near him was a wooden container with shelves holding tools and maybe there was a cupboard underneath. Also near was a large terra-cotta jar (known as a crock) containing a noxious looking fluid; it was only water but had become dyed dark brown from the pieces of leather that were soaked in it. Under the counter there were shelves that held rolls of leather. At the back of the workshop were shelves on which stood "lasts" wooden models of customers feet used in making "made to measure" shoes. He also made what he uncompromisingly called "cripple boots". The craft had its own vocabulary, the "uppers" were the soft tops to the shoes and these were usually made by a different craftsman; sometimes if they were "brogues" they were decorated with a narrow border of cut out round holes. Sometimes we would go and collect the uppers from Sharpes warehouse. Sharpes had a shop in the Promenade, the one which still has a fine decorative iron balcony, and behind in County Court Road, they had a workshop. This was long and narrow and presided over by a foreman wearing, over his suit, an apron down to his ankles and a bowler hat. Later my mother would rent part of these premises as her first dancing school.

Sometimes a friend would sit and talk to my grandfather, selling him produce from his garden. Once we were all amused when after a whole summer of buying rhubarb which had by that time become coarse and green, he asked, in his rather lugubrious voice "Would you like some rhubarb?", as though it was the greatest treat in the world.

It must have been shortly before World War II another man joined my grandfather; he was a doctor displaced from somewhere in Eastern Europe. He was giving his services in return for instruction on how to make shoes, probably I should think "cripple boots". After a while he stopped coming and some years later returned to Eastern Europe. Who knows what political machinations went on there, but we were all sorry to know that he met an untimely end.

The corridor down the side of the workshop led to the hallway at the bottom of a flight of stairs. Here there stood a piece of furniture now singularly defunct - a hall stand. This one was made of dark wood with a mirror and places to put umbrellas and walking sticks, and a lot of pegs on which to hang coats. At one time a straw "boater" hat hung on one of the hooks with a stiff white collar round it. It was said that once

Amina with her Elston grandparents

in an absent-minded moment my grandfather had gone out wearing the hat still adorned with the collar.

Stairs led to the kitchen and scullery below down in the basement. The kitchen had a large table, the usual built-in dresser and a pair of old steps, like stairs, which had once been used for getting into high Victorian beds. In the scullery there was a cylindrical boiler, and an iron mangle. The light was fairly dim and originally the artificial light would have been by gas mantle. The daylight came through the window which was enclosed by a skylight in which there was said to live a toad called Tomogos.

Back at the hall stand a door led into the living room where there were two chairs one on each side of the fireplace, a sideboard and a high cabinet, strangely said to have been made out of an old upright piano. The table was fairly large and only one of the leaves was open, later when it filtered down to me, I should find that it was a Regency Pembroke table they had purchased from an old man who had it from the Fleece Hotel, in the lower High Street, where it had been used with others fastened together (with little brass bolts underneath) to make a very long and large table at which farmers attending the weekly market would take their lunch. On a wall there was also a well known sentimental Victorian print of a large and a small dog called "Dignity and Impudence". Times could be hard and I know that there were sometimes days when they sat at that table with only bread and cheese for their lunch.

My grandmother was a dressmaker but she no longer had the roomful of "girls" that had once inhabited an upstairs room, though I was familiar with the old fashioned Singer treadle sewing machine that they had

Amina and grandfather Elston

used. My mother used to say that as a child one of her games had been to take round the little drawers, built into the ends of the machine to hold spools of thread, elastic and so on, to "sell" to the girls, a form of playing "shop". At one point in her life my grandmother had been head of the workroom at Shires and Lances and in those days was paid I think it was 15/- a week. (At that time an average wage per week for a man was about 15/-, doubtless women's wages were less, so as head of the workroom she earned about the same as a man.)

My grandparent's house was opposite the Female Orphan Asylum in Winchcombe Street. When the orphans went on their annual holiday my grandmother, often with me in tow, went over to feed their cats. It was a large building with echoing wooden floors. I can still smell the freshly scrubbed pine tables in the kitchen where we mashed up the white fish, great collops that would cost a fortune today.

At the back there was a large playground with a few fowls railed in to one area. We used to throw them maize among the sweet smelling rosemary and fennel bushes.

Winchcombe Street was one of dwelling houses with the occasional "corner shop" interspersed with the small premises of craftsmen. As well as my grandfathers little shop, there was also at least one saddler, perhaps two, and on the opposite side of the street the School for the Blind where they made baskets.

There was also a Chinese laundry, as far as I know then the only Chinese business in the town. It was where one sent one's best washing like dress shirts. It was my grandmother who, if something was delayed and failed to come back on time learnt the term "ee-come ee-come", that passed into the family's vocabulary.

Sometimes my grandmother would take me down to the grocers halfway down the street, which stood out from a regency terrace. There was a great mound of butter on one of the counters where one's purchase was cut off and beaten up into shape with a pair of ribbed wooden bats (butter pats) and, I think for my benefit, it would sometimes be formed into a round shape and the picture of a cow impressed into the top. It was the only shop I ever remember where there was still sawdust over the floor.

Further down the street was Lockes Bakery and Drakes Store where we sometimes went to buy dress fabric. When you paid for your purchase the bill and the money were put into a long thin container which was placed in a hole in the wall where it was whizzed up to the office and would shortly return with the receipt and the change. The Famous was still using this system as late as 2008, I think as a tribute to the past. they continued to use them until they shut on January 5th 2013.

The Famous, a men's outfitters, was in the High Street and as a toddler I occasionally went there with my grandmother. We would go upstairs where the tailors sat cross-legged on a large table and my grandmother would ask them to work some buttonholes for her. She could work her own buttonholes but tailor's were better.

I do not think it was very often but sometimes my grandfather would take me to the Horse Repository, half way down Winchcombe Street where the horses were trotted round in a small circle to be auctioned.

I think he must have put me on his shoulders because it seemed that I looked down on to a sea of bowler hats and flat caps. The building had been the showroom of Miles the coach builder, but by my time this was gone.

A more regular outing was on Sunday mornings when he would call for me and we would walk together to Hewlett Road where his brother Harry had a little sweet shop and they would chat while I made a lengthy choice of some sweets or a bar of chocolate. I could buy a pennyworth of sweets served in a cone of paper, but my mother said when she was young you could get four different sorts for a penny, a farthing's worth of each.

We had special treats at Christmas time, on Boxing Day my grandfather would take me to see the Meet of the Hunt outside the Queen's Hotel. All up the Promenade people would be waiting at the edge of the road and we would watch the beautiful horses and men in pink coats with the hounds go by. Some of the ladies rode side saddle wearing black habits, top hats and veils. After drinking a stirrup cup they would all trot down the Promenade again; it was a great event, much enjoyed by everyone.

There is an elaborate fountain in the Promenade with a statue of Neptune and sea-horses, my grandfather could remember the man who modelled for Neptune, and many years later he would tell me that the man's name was Robin, though whether this was his Christian or surname I do not know. He was known as "Cock-Robin" because of his prowess with the ladies.

Another annual event was my grandmother taking me to Gloucester. We usually went by train and she carried a holly wreath to put on her sister Sally's grave. After we had visited the cemetery we went to the Bon Marché, had something to eat, and I would be taken to Santa's grotto, before going home by train. In those days they were proper trains, towering above you and emitting whistles and steam in all directions.

My grandfather's father had been a journeyman boot maker, from Devon I believe, and when he married, he and his wife had six sons and two daughters. They seem, very sensibly, to have operated their own personal apprenticeship scheme; all the boys were either tailors or shoemakers and the older ones trained the younger ones.

As a young man my grandfather was sent to London to train with one of his elder brothers. He used to recall how he had seen the remnants of the Light Brigade, who made the famous, or should I say infamous, charge during the Crimean War, sitting at some celebrations in Hyde Park. Also how Queen Victoria had driven past him in an open carriage and made him a little bow while he stood at the side of the road and took off his bowler hat to her.

Cars had no place in my grandparent's life but bicycles did. My grandfather must have been fairly athletic in his youth, he had gone in for walking races and also recalled the racing by "tall bikes" (commonly called penny-farthings) in Montpellier Gardens.

In their early married life they seem to have taken to bicycles in the big way. They rode out into the country, sometimes down to Lower Lode by the river at Tewkesbury. When my mother was a small child they had a caneware carriage for her which was attached behind one of the bicycles, and her feet rested on the picnic basket. To the end of his life my grandfather thought that the nicest outfit that a woman could wear was a long dark skirt, a white blouse, doubtless with "leg of mutton" sleeves and a straw boater hat.

My grandmother, whose maiden name was Webb, had been born in the Forest of Dean. She had a brother who was a baker and three sisters, Sally who married a man from Gloucester, a butcher I believe; Kate who emigrated with her husband Jack Dodwell to Toronto and Jinny who married Alf Trunkfield and emigrated to Vancouver. "Trunki", as they called him, had been in the cavalry in the First World War and I remember him saying that when they had to make a charge he would put his head down by his horse's neck, stick his sword out in front and shut his eyes.

Years later the Trunkfields would visit us when they had a chain of grocery stores. It was after World War II but food was still rationed. Trunkfield was a self entitled "meat eater" and any form of salad he regarded as "rabbit food". They brought a cabin-trunk full of food with them, but even so there was a certain resentment when he completely and obliviously ate every ones weeks ration of bacon for his breakfast one morning.

My Father's Parents.

I did not know my father's parents, they died before I was born. The Chatwins came from Birmingham industry, his father Walter was an accountant with the family firm. Walter's father was Thomas, a mechanical engineer who lived at The Vale in Edgbaston and owned the Victoria Work's in Great Tindal Street making stocks, dies and taps. The work had been awarded medals at exhibitions in Calcutta in 1884, Stockholm, 1886, Adelaide, 1887 and Melbourne in 1889.

My grandfather Walter married Susannah, née Jackson, of a family of yeomen farmers on the Cotswolds. As a young woman she had gone to Birmingham and worked in an office, whether this was the Chatwin office I do not know, but when the marriage took place it was generally thought that Walter had "married beneath him". Susannah had a brother Fred who worked Upcote Farm near Withington. Once in the fields he had fallen and broken one of his legs and by the time he had crawled back to the farm the bone was sticking out of the skin. Their wedding group was photographed in front of the farm and it was obviously an important occasion.

All the ladies were wearing enormous fashionable circular hats. Walter's sister Amina, I was named after her, was there but I am not sure that I see any other member of the Chatwin family.

The grass in the front of the house is clearly very long, the first lawn mower had been invented by Edwin Budding in 1830 at the Phoenix Works in Thrupp, Stroud, which was not far away, but they were obviously not yet in use on the local farms.

Walter and Susannah set up home, I was once told "in some style" in King's Norton, where my father, Walter Vincent, their only child, was born in 1899. It would have been a very different home to that of my Elston grandparents. From the few possessions that have come down to me I know there would have been fine china, silverware, and good antique furniture and clocks.

Later they lived in the Cotswolds, certainly at Stockwell Farm near Birdlip. It was probably Stockwell of which we had a photograph, with an open carriage drawn up in front of it; and doubtless from there that my father used to daily walk two miles each way to school at Cowley. He once told me that he used to like to go to a rise in the Gloucester to Cirencester road near a public house called "The Golden Hart" in Nettleton Bottom, to see if any of the cars, then beginning to come on to the roads, would break down on the hill. If they did he would help to push them up and hopefully be rewarded by a ride in the vehicle.

The last place they lived was Ingleside on Crickley Hill and my father finished his schooling at Northfield House in Cheltenham. Towards the end of the First World War he spent a short time in the RAF. I never heard anything about it except that he was once given the job of doling out stew to a vast number of servicemen on Salisbury Plain; it was then that he learnt a salutary lesson - there was sufficient except that there was none left for him!

His interest in cars was clearly forward looking, so it is no surprise that he was not drawn either to craftsmanship or industry but to a new 20th century occupation - he trained with Marconi as a wireless operator and joined the British Merchant Marine.

He certainly achieved a motorcycle by this time as I have a small photograph of him on it outside the house on Crickley Hill.

His mother became very ill in 1920 and by May her sisters were rallying round to look after her. She wrote a letter to her son on May 8th, "Aunt Evelyn went away today and Aunt Selina just arrived". They were hoping that "Aunt Ida will bring a nurse from Cirencester next week".

She was very weak but "still hoping to see you when you reach Glasgow". This was not to be as she died nine days later, aged only 54. The letter was the last he ever received from her and he kept it throughout his life.

Dad on motorcycle

My father must have been home for a while the following year as he took photographs at Browns Farm the home of his Aunt Ida. They show a shooting party, an unknown man, with my father, and a lanky schoolboy, Dudley. A younger son was Tim, who later became a baker at the best cake shop in Cheltenham (Maison Kunz, run by a Swiss, Mr Krier) and during World War II a fireman. There is also a photograph of my grandfather Chatwin; he is no longer the confident dark haired man at the centre of the wedding photograph, he has white hair, a large white moustache and a lost look. It is not surprising, he had lost his dearly beloved wife and his son was usually far away. He spent the end of his life staying at The Cross Hands in Brockworth. I have heard he was sometimes over fond of brandy, but who can blame him, it must have been the only comfort he had left.

Walter Chatwin

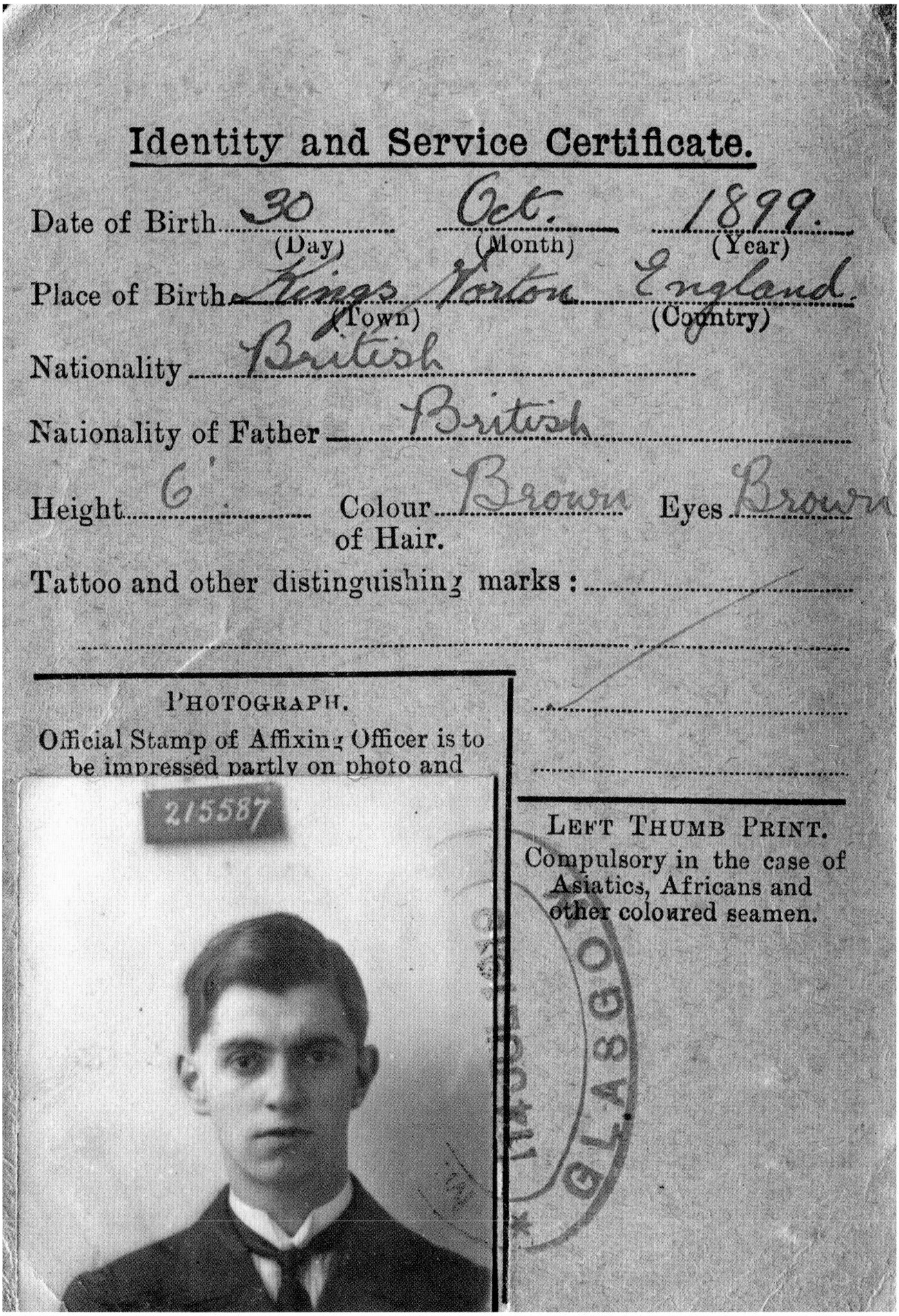

Identity and Service Certificate.

Date of Birth _30_ _Oct._ _1899._
     (Day)   (Month)   (Year)

Place of Birth _Kings Norton_ _England._
      (Town)   (Country)

Nationality _British_

Nationality of Father _British_

Height _6'_   Colour _Brown_   Eyes _Brown_
       of Hair.

Tattoo and other distinguishing marks : _____

_____

PHOTOGRAPH.

Official Stamp of Affixing Officer is to
be impressed partly on photo and

215587

LEFT THUMB PRINT.
Compulsory in the case of
Asiatics, Africans and
other coloured seamen.

GLASGOW

25

My Father at Sea.

I have a small photograph album made during my father's early years at sea. An Arab woman in a street in Algiers, temples in India, and an ox-cart in Calcutta. There are beach scenes in Saint-Malo and the docks at Dunkirk in 1921, and the Gatun and Pacific locks on the Panama Canal. The following year there are the Bengal Lancers riding along a path beside a river and timber elephants working in Moulmein, Burma.

Walter Vincent Chatwin
in 1921 at Dunkirk

Panama Canal
in early 1920's

There are a number of ships some of which he must have served on; he was on the Constadt in 1920-21, then the SS City of Calcutta, a passenger liner, from August 1921, which I think plied between Bombay and Calcutta. He was on the SS Warina in 1922-23. He wrote to his Aunt Ida in June 1923 saying . . .

SS City of Calcutta

"We are now quite settled down to the run between here and Bangkok (as far as I know until next spring). I like this part of the world quite well and have no desire to return to India". He then describes a visit to a friend who was second assistant on a rubber estate; it covered about 5,000 acres and the friend looked after 1,200 of them, the only European on the section. He was in charge of 200 Tamil labourers. He describes the average day in a planter's life: -

"You rise at 5 a.m. have a cold bath and a cup of tea and toast and at 5.30 muster the coolies (Note. The word "Coolie" was always used to denote an Indian or Chinese hired labourer, in recent dictionaries the word is said to be offensive but presumably this is only if it is applied to someone who is not a hired labourer. AC.), and get them to work. Then follows about half an hours work in the office, after that you get round the section and keep shaking up the weeding coolies, at 9 a.m. you make for your bungalow and have breakfast (you usually feel like it believe me) from 10 to 12 there are many jobs about the estate to keep one busy, at 12 noon the coolies begin to come in with the latex (rubber sap) that has to be checked and put into tanks which takes until 2 p.m. (Later he adds "To see them bringing in the latex reminds you of a dairy for it looks like milk".) that is your days work finished unless something exceptional is being done. You then have tiffin and a couple of hours sleep. Then tea and after that pass away the time in whatever way you think fit, on two or three nights a week most of the chaps go to the club and play tennis until dark and then bridge etc until about 9 p.m. You may have dinner any time between then and 1 a.m. according to what you are doing, it is wonderful how these Chinese boys make up dinner when you arrive at your bungalow about 11 p.m. with three or four unexpected guests. One night Reid, another fellow and myself thought we would visit a chap about fifteen miles away in a rather lonely place, we arrived about 9.30 and by about 10.15 his boy had a slap up dinner ready for the lot of us, yet when we arrived he was only making it for one. Of course you can see from this that bed time is very elastic. Practically all the fellows have motor bikes and the older married men etc cars. Taking it all round it is not a bad sort of life, (much better than being at sea)."

He speaks of a tiger taking one of the dogs from outside the bungalow, and of snakes, Cobras and King Cobras, one they had recently killed had been seventeen and a half feet long and six inches in diameter. It is clear from this letter that he was thinking that he might return to the East as a planter.

A Typhoon in the China Sea.

He also left a vivid account of a China Sea typhoon that passed over Hong Kong on the morning of August 18th 1923. . .

"All ships were instructed to leave their moorings in the harbour and anchor in the typhoon anchorage, this we did at 6 p.m.

At 10 pm, all was still and not a ripple broke the surface of the water, though there was a very ominous looking sky away to the north east. At 4 a.m. the wind was coming up in very vicious gusts and it was clear that we were in for something of a fairly severe character, and by 6.30 it had freshened to a howling N E gale. By 8.30 the wind had practically reached typhoon force, and was increasing all the time, accompanied by very heavy rain.

By 9 a.m. the saloon and all our rooms were leaking badly and by 9.30 everything was soaking and there was about two inches of water in our rooms. The Hong Kong observatory then fired three explosive signals, which meant that the typhoon was expected to strike Hong Kong in about half an hour.

By 10 a.m. it was indescribable, the wind was incomprehensibly terrific, rain was falling and spray was lifted in sheets and the sound was like a number of locomotives blowing off and whistling all at the same time, and it was quite impossible to see for more than a hundred yards. We had our two anchors out and were not only steaming full ahead, but all we could do, to try and ease the tremendous strain on our cables, but even then we were dragging our anchors. The wind then tore away a part of the tarpaulin on No 2 hatch, so I decided that I had better get on deck and give what help I could, as a coat was useless I went out as I was in a shirt and shorts, I was no sooner on deck when the wind took me clean off my feet, it was quite impossible to stand or walk without hanging on to something, and by the time I reached the hatch my shirt was away in about five pieces. The 3rd officer myself and four men started to try and make fast the tarpaulin but our efforts were worse than useless until we got all hands on to it, and then we had a hard fight of it for three-quarters of an hour before we got it made fast. We then got rather a shock, for suddenly a ship (name unknown) came flying past missing us by only a few yards, she was almost on her beam ends having a starboard list of fully forty degrees, and had lost her anchors and cables and her engines did not appear to be working.

A few minutes later the SS Lama drifted very close to us, dragging her anchors although she was steaming full ahead.

The centre of the typhoon then passed over and for a few minutes it was dead calm except for the heavy sea that was running, then the wind changed to the other quarter and came on again with the same relentless fury as before.

A raft with ten men passed us but we could not help them in any way, the poor beggars looked the picture of misery. About noon the wind started to decrease in force and by 1.30 things were fairly safe again, we had drifted well over a mile. The Rhiems, the Cheekeeang, the Hop On and many other ships were on the rocks on Stonecutters Island, and the ship that nearly hit us was on Green Island. The Loomsang had sunk, her masts and funnel were just visible above the surface. One of her life boats and a raft were trying to make for one of the other ships and after a long fight managed to get picked up.

We sailed at 5 p.m. for Bangkok all feeling sore stiff and tired, but thankful we had got off so much better than some of the others.

Later reports state that the typhoon was the most severe since 1906, when 10,000 lives were lost in Hong Kong in two hours.

The lives lost amounted to 60, only two Europeans were saved off the Loomsang, the rest and also the wife of the 2nd engineer who was on board at the time were lost. Besides this twenty ships were driven on to the rocks, most of them being badly damaged.

The velocity of the wind was at times 130 miles per hour which is probably a world record. The barometer fell to 28.66 which is the lowest reading ever recorded in Hong Kong. Damage done on shore amounted to several million dollars worth."

My Father Leaves the Sea.

My father left the sea in 1924 but evidently thought better of returning to the east as a planter. It must have been somewhere around this time that he met my mother so perhaps that had something to do with the change of plan.

When my mother was still a child she was a member of the "Butterfly and Wasp" troupe. We know from newspaper cuttings and memorabilia collected by my grandfather that they sometimes performed at the Baker-street Institute, Cheltenham, when "Miss P. Elston gave her very graceful solo dances and also for a Dutch dance in costume in which master E. Norris took part and then "The full strength of the troupe was heard in the familiar strains of 'Swanee Ribber' (no such thing as political correctness then) and the choruses to which mandolins, castanets and tambourins added pleasing variety." Whether this was instrumental in inspiring her to a life of dance I do not know, but she was set on it and really never wavered throughout her life. In 1921 she went to stay with relatives in London in order to study at the Lillie and Grace Cone School of Dancing. When she successfully passed her Association of Operatic Dancing of Great Britain examination, among the judges were Madam Tamar Karsavina and Miss Phyllis Bedells, both very well known dancers of their time.

My father was articled as a pupil and assistant for ten years with Rainger and Rogers Architects. Cheltenham, in December 1924.

I expect he learnt to dance and the first time he met my mother's father was when he went into the shop to ask him if he would stitch a tear in the hood of his car. My grandfather did not like the sound of the job and said his machine was out of order; so the first meeting with his future son-in-law was not particularly auspicious. Things must have progressed satisfactorily, however, as at some point, in a year or two, they evidently all went away on a holiday together - I know this because there is a photograph of them on a beach.

It is at this point that I begin to wonder if I was conceived in the sand hills; it was many years later that I noticed when looking at their wedding certificate and my birth certificate that they were married on January 31st 1927 and I was born at the end of March. I had always been told that I was born prematurely and it may have been the case but it must have been very inconvenient as it looks as if it was a close run thing anyway! You may say this sort of thing did not happen in the twenties - but I think it did!

However there was nothing hole-in-the-corner about the wedding it took place at the parish church, and there must have been friends and relatives attending as at 5.15 on the same day my father sent a postcard to grandmother Elston:-

"Just arrived at Goodrich. It seems quite a nice little place. Hope everything went off O.K. Just going to have some tea, Phyll says she is hungry."

It was probably before her marriage that my mother was doing exhibition dances with Jack Morgan at the Town Hall Thé Dansant performing the Tango, Du Rêve, and the latest Riviera Valse. For 2/6 one could obtain full entry to both tea and dancing, or tea was 1/6; spectators could sit in the balcony for 4d including tax.

I think my mother hankered after a stage career and probably soon after their marriage persuaded (for I am sure that must have been the way of it) my father to tour the L.M.S. hotels with her, when they performed the minuet, waltz, gavotte and polka, in historical costume. I rather wonder if it was the loss of this dream that led her to have what was in those days known as "a nervous breakdown", I think she continued teaching but was apprehensive about going out. I should think I was about three or four when I used to go with her and my grandmother (always such a supporting figure) when they would sit beside the Old Winter Garden that used to stand behind the Town Hall in Imperial Gardens, and I would play on the grass. I think it was part of the rehabilitation regime.

On the whole I seem to remember less about where I lived in the early years than about my grandparents and Winchcombe Street. I recall looking out of the living room window with my parents [1932] and being told to look upwards to see a Zeppelin in the sky. On another, occasion, probably some years later, we were listening to a fracas going on beyond our garden. An alleyway led through from the Bath Road to a low building belonging to next door, I think perhaps it had been a private chapel or showroom for Boulton's the stonemasons who had once lived in the house next to ours. Near the building the inhabitants from the little house next to the alley appeared to be beating something on the floor with a cricket bat, surely they were not beating an animal!

Well it shows the way things must have been in those days because after a while we heard a voice and I said "Oh, its all right it's only an Irishman"!

Another night from the same window there was a very fine show of the aurora borealis lighting up the whole sky with colours.

I had few outings with my father except that often on a Sunday afternoon all three of us would drive to one of the surrounding hills, Cleeve or Leckhampton and go for a walk. My father used to point out the fossils and I early learnt that the Cotswolds had long ago been under the sea. On one memorable occasion, after my mother had been ill with flu and I had been "good". he took me to Woolworths and bought me anything in which I expressed an interest. I remember a small white teddy bear, for which I was really too old and some thin books, largely illustrating history.

At one time he would go early morning cold swimming at the Alstone baths and sometimes bring back lovely new, practically still hot, currant dripping cakes for our breakfast. Another of his interests was motor cycle football and going on motor cycle scrambles.

Another thing he sometimes brought in of an evening were faggots and peas made by an ample lady who kept a small vegetable shop in Cambray. There was a good fish and chip shop on the other side of the road by the Garrick's Head, the local public house favoured by my father and when he came to live with us, my grandfather also, for their evening pint.

"Old Clapp" had an electricity shop in Cambray and workshops all down a narrow alleyway behind it. Later the shop specialised in lamp shades under the guardianship of "Young Clapp".

On the corner of Cambray and Wellington Street was a piece of waste ground known as "the Cabbage Patch". A woman was murdered there once but violence was a rare happening, on the whole the streets were safe and quiet and one walked without fear. Even after the war started I was in the Red Cross Cadets and would walk down to the Old Gloucester Road to the headquarters without apprehension.

In the early days there was a row of trees opposite our house and a field. It must have been slightly too small for a tennis court because at one time my father thought of buying it for that purpose but found it was not quite large enough. They used to go and play tennis up by the brick-works in Leckhampton. Sometimes Boulton used the field, when a very old man, with a sack over his shoulders, used to sit and saw tomb stones all day. Once when my mother had been ill for a day or two she found it very depressing, hearing him there in the gently falling rain.

As a small child I was not taken out much after dark but I do remember how exciting I found the High Street when the shops were lit up. In those days the shop keepers used to hang quite a lot of things outside the shop fronts, it might be clothes or food - butchers displayed meat or chickens on hooks; fish shops had display slabs facing on to the street with all the different kinds of fish laid out. Tramcars would rush up and down the street ringing bells and with sparks flying - it was exciting.

There was a shop called G.H. New who sold Indian and Chinese tea and things imported from Japan. Best of all, they sold something dear to my heart, if things were going well, whoever I was with could sometimes be persuaded to take me inside and buy something small and dry, heaven knows what it was, but one took it home and then the delight happened. The small dry bits had to be dropped into a cup or bowl of water and then the little bits opened out into soft colourful shapes like flowers. I cannot remember how long they lasted and I do not know to this day what they were or where they came from.

On the other side of the High Street was a branch of the Cadena and later when I started going to school one of my friends had her parties there. I would go wearing a party dress and a cherry red velvet cloak lined with white satin sprigged with flowers. When it came to tea I was careful to sit near a plate of sardine sandwiches and slowly eat my way through them, ladies leant over me proffering a variety of cakes but I was deaf to their entreaties, sardine sandwiches were my favourite food!

I particularly enjoyed May 1st because on that day the cart horses, and there were quite a few of them in those days, wore all their brightly polished horse brasses. They certainly drew coal wagons and, I think beer drays. Ponies delivered milk in little carts and in the earlier days the milkmen had a large churn or can on the cart from which they ladled milk into the house holder's jug.

In 1935, when I was eight years old, the Lido, or open-air swimming pool, was opened in Cheltenham and I was roped in by Gough and Edwards, a store in the High Street, (Numbers 404-5-6 on the south side) to be a child model. I wore a bathing costume and carried a bucket and spade and towelling cloak, accompanying three lady models.

Beauty contest at the Lido with Amina aged eight

I went to a small private school situated at first in the Bath Road almost opposite the turning to St. Luke's Road. I remember that at assembly we sat on the floor and learnt about the British Empire. When I first went there it was run by two elderly ladies called The Misses Jewell. By the time I walked to school alone I went up Wellington Street past the stonemasons R.L. Boulton & Sons. The pavements were covered with white stone dust and one could see all sorts of work going on inside. Further up the street were four cottages where "Skipper Sardines" lived, so called by me because one of the inhabitants had a beard and wore a sou'wester rain hat like that favoured by the man on the front of the well known brand of sardines. Then came the River Chelt; by craning up and standing on one's toes it was possible to look down over the wall to the water and sometimes to see a duck or two. It would have been about here that earlier, before the houses in the street were built, there had been a stone monument in the form of an obelisk in the gardens of Wellington Mansion that stood in Cambray and looked down towards the river.

After the bridge was a house that laid back and later after World War II started it would be filled with evacuees who were dearly loved by the lady who owned the house and she kept in touch with them for many years. Opposite were two houses in one of which lived the chef from the Ellenbrough Hotel (on Oriel Road at the top of the street) and he, being in the Home Guard, would teach us all how to put out incendiary bombs with a bucket and a stirrup pump. The family in the basement of the house next to us left me with an abiding hatred of Jehovah's Witnesses because they refused to join our group of fire watchers, saying God would look after them, and it obviously did not matter about the rest of us. The owner of that house walked with difficulty, apparently he had been lying wounded in no-man's land during the First World War and a German had come along and broken both his legs, presumably he had later been rescued and survived.

Then came a long terrace of Regency houses. Later I would know the people in the last one. The old gentleman worked in my father's office (who was by then head of Vale & Kingsford in Gloucester). The interior was Dickensian with the living room walls covered with red flock wallpaper and I think there was even a cloth pelmet hanging from the mantelpiece above the fire, as in the Victorian period. The lady of the house had also been a dressmaker and had a workroom leading off from the top of the staircase which had also once contained "girls" and treadle sewing machines.

The first floor was let to a little lady from the Channel Islands whose daughter Olive Blackham ran a marionette show for adults from her home in the granary of Roel Farm near Guiting Power. When the war started she came into Cheltenham and took a job at Lloyds Bank. At some point she started teaching a small group of people how to make papier mâché puppet heads and that was my first introduction to a new and exciting world.

A friend of Olive's lived in the next house that faced onto Oriel Road, with her nephew. The boy's parents had been returning from abroad at the beginning of the war when they were torpedoed and spent many days with others in an open boat, until one night they went quietly over the side together, to leave more food for the remaining survivors.

The school must have still been in Bath Road during the war because I remember coming out one afternoon and, with a couple of friends, standing watching a dog fight going on in the sky overhead, until one of the teachers came out and told us to go home.

In 1940, there was an air-raid on Coventry by 500 planes and 568 people were killed.

It was in January 1940 that we had a strange ice storm. I could see from the moment I woke up, in my little room at the top of the house that something was unusual. In those days it was possible to see some poplar trees from the window and they were a strange shape. Instead of sticking straight up their boughs spread out sideways and downwards in a very unusual way. When I walked to school I passed a laurel bush and found that every leaf was encased in ice with a hard drop of ice at the end of each. I have never seen such a thing either before or since. The rain froze as it fell encasing everything in ice, even the birds sitting on telegraph wires and trees.

The school was taken over by one of the younger teachers and moved to Fairholme, Montpellier Drive, and later moved to Southam but by that time I had left.

At some point my mother thought it would be a good thing for me to go as a day girl to the Ladies College. My parents were looked into and passed as suitable, for they were in professions, though I am rather surprised that a dancing teacher was considered suitable. All began to be prepared and my uniform, I remember dresses of small green check cotton for summer, to be made ready. Then the blow fell, it would not after all be possible for me to go. They had discovered, it had certainly not occurred to us to tell them, that my mother's father had his little shoe shop in Winchcombe Street and they could not possibly have anything to do with trade. I am surprised that such an attitude lasted into the first half of the 20th century. I believe that the Gentleman's College had the same rule which is why Dean Close School was formed where they were not so adverse to trade. It did not worry me at the time, but looking back I can see it probably meant that I lost any chance of a better education than I received. In those days no one ever mentioned university you did not go there unless you were very clever, and preferably male, or had a lot of money. A few men got to university from grammar schools but the attitude was by no means the same as it is today.

ORIEL SCHOOL HOCKEY TEAM, which won all its matches this term, scoring 30 goals to four. Back row, left to right: G. Diekenson, M. Clarke, A. Chatwin, B. Haward, K. Weston, P. Griffiths. Seated: S. Sheen, J. Bick, P. Christopher (captain), M. Bourne, V. Phelps.

Taken in 1942

One of my friends Joy Bick (who died suddenly in May 2013), used to ride her pony to school each day and leave it at the vets in St. James's Square. Later it was replaced with a bicycle which was left at garages opposite Leslie Paynter's motor cycle shop on the corner of Cambray and Wellington Street. My friend would call for me and we would walk up to school together. The war would catch up with us and she would leave school at sixteen to help on her parent's farm by which time it would be largely worked by Italian prisoners of war. I remained a little longer at school training to take my qualification as a Licentiate of the Guildhall School of Music and Drama so that I could introduce speech training at my mother's dancing school.

The three graces, which include Amina and her mother

I was always interested in books and from an early age used to go after school, to a second-hand bookshop in Pittville Street (Rawlins) and buy books for 3d and 6d each. We had a good grounding in Shakespeare at school and Donald Wolfit brought his company fairly frequently to the "Opera House" and we were always taken in a group from school to see the performances.

One of my friends used to live in The Old Manor, Chester Walk, and another in Royal Crescent where we used to play in what was then a private garden in the middle of the crescent, and is now the centre of the bus station.

If I think of food both before and after the war, I can see that the standard menu for the middle classes was roast meat on Sundays, cold on Mondays, followed by the meat minced, then perhaps fish, eggs or liver and bacon or sometimes rabbit or a joint of boiled bacon. A rare treat would be steak and kidney pie or pudding (my grandfather used to recall the latter as individual "Babies-heads" served in London Steak Houses in his youth). Chicken would be something of a treat for Sunday lunch at intervals or for celebrations. The first course would be followed if you were lucky by a milk pudding, rice, semolina, bread and butter, or the revolting glutinous tapioca or sago. If whoever was doing the cooking was in a good mood, there might be a suet pudding, jam roly-poly or a spotted dick, or apples in a suet crust. Strange how tastes change, the small potatoes that my grandmother used to call "Pig potatoes" (fit only for the pigs), and at one point in the First World War the only thing obtainable, are now luxury "baby new potatoes"

It was on September 3rd 1939 that World War II started. We had been on our annual holiday, this time to North Wales, and came back a day early to start putting up some blackout. In the days that followed we bought lots of black cotton fabric to line curtains with and stuck paper tape criss-crossed over the window panes in the hope of preventing broken glass from falling out and cutting passers-by. There was a great influx of people into the town, not only evacuees but servicemen and factories from London. For the grown-up inhabitants of the town it could never have been the same again. My parents used to go to the Saturday night dances at the Town Hall wearing evening dress, but in a year or two it would be Rock-and-Roll and casual dress for everyone.

I would have been twelve at the beginning of the war when my mother's parents left their little shop in Winchcombe Street and moved into the basement of our house. After a while I did the shopping and cooking, and at night we all slept in the basement in case of air raids; then my father, who by this time was a quantity surveyor, left to build aerodromes in the Midlands around Stoke-on-Trent. Where he stayed at first must have been pretty rough because I remember him telling me that he had to be careful at meal times that the men sitting each side of him did not steal the food off his plate. I expect he told this to the Clerk-of-Works because he was invited to go and stay with him and his wife at Meir Heath and they all became life-long friends.

I remember taking the train to visit him sitting on the floor of the guard's van. All trains were incredibly crowded and soldiers were often passed horizontally through the tiny top windows if it was absolutely necessary that they should get into the train. My mother going to London during the time of the flying bombs (heaven knows why) travelled packed into a lavatory with several men. People stood everywhere, all the corridors were packed as were the stations. One is tempted to ask why my mother was travelling to London at a time of such great danger; it could only have been to examine dance medals or go to a conference, but there was a kind of pride in living ones usual life and not letting them get the better of us. In London she would stay with some friends where the mother was blind, and they spent horrific nights in a little house in Shepherd's Bush that was next door to a very tall block of flats fearing that the building would be brought down on top of them. We called the flying bombs "Doodle-bugs or "Buzz-bombs", they looked like aircraft but were unmanned and were really one large bomb with wings on. I cannot remember just when, but after the bombing had gone on for a year or two the Germans started using these unmanned rockets to bomb us. They were not guided, just aimed in their general direction and sent off, some nine thousand people in London were killed by them.

On one occasion I visited my father in the Midlands. Sometimes in the evenings, unless the men were trout fishing at the pool, we would go for a walk. Once we followed a path through the woods beside a stream where there were a series of little deserted workshops. We went into one where the door was open, it was as if the work force had just walked out, there were still jobs half done on the benches, even some tools and work-coats hanging behind the door - the men had departed. It did not occur to me at the time but looking back I wonder where they were, in the deserts of Egypt or the jungles of Burma perhaps, for our men fought in many theatres of war. One day my father took me to Etruria to go round the Wedgwood factory to see the pottery being made, which I found extremely interesting.

Once my father took me into the local public house where there was a back room where regulars used to foregather. Had I but known it there was a young man there that I should look for practically all my life and not find until it was too late. As a young engineer he would shortly be sent into France before Dunkirk, with a small group of soldiers to identify and bring back machine tools for making prototype guns for use in aircraft, to prevent them falling into enemy hands. A film "The Foreman went to France" was made by Ealing Studios of this episode in 1941. It was based on the exploits of Melbourne Johns so presumably he was in charge and the man who later become my friend, must have been a smaller cog in the wheel. It must, however, have been a dangerous mission since he was technically a civilian and if he had been captured he would have been regarded as a spy. By the time of D Day he was involved with a pipe line that took petrol across the Channel.

I think it must have been shortly before the war that my father learnt to fly. He used to take my mother to asparagus suppers at the aerodrome. When the war came he was anxious to join a group of ladies and older men who ferried aircraft, which had landed up at the wrong airfields, to where they were needed. It was sometime around this time when walking down the High Street that I saw Amy Johnson drive a car into the entrance of the Plough Hotel. She was famous for her solo flights across the world and once the war started she was part of the group ferrying planes, and lost her life when she was brought down over the Channel in 1941.

Cheltenham was not heavily bombed, but nightly our fire fighters travelled to Bristol, Birmingham or Coventry to fight the terrible conflagrations and devastation caused by the bombing. Once my mother came hurriedly into the living room from her bedroom saying "Oh a bomb just went down the street!" It is possible that it practically did as that night a house was taken out in Parabola Road [Bayshill Road] and two in the Tivoli area, which were all very close. For the most part the bombing was confined to some small streets near the railway line in the lower part of the town. Pilley Bridge was destroyed by a direct hit, and would not be rebuilt for fourteen years. The worst night was on December 11th 1940 when 2000 incendiary and 155 high explosive bombs were dropped causing 23 fatalities. The Sunningend aircraft works and the gas works were set on fire, 400 houses damaged, and 600 people made homeless. Perhaps it was the night that "Grandma Jane Norris" who lived in the top flat next door, and was Ewart's mother, tottered in saying "I thought I had better come in because things started falling off the mantelpiece."

There were dark days when we waited to be invaded and I took care to know where the bread knife, which was remarkably like a Roman short sword, was kept, so that I could get my hands on it if necessary.

My father set up targets on the top of the rockery and we learnt to shoot at them from the area in the basement, using his sporting gun.

They must have been desperate times. We knew a young Midshipman who was sent one night into the hills behind Portsmouth, with a few sailors and told to "defend the country".

All through the town there were little workshops set up making spare parts for aircraft. There was one next door that had been an upholsterers. On the other side of the road was another building where the parts were kept and given out by a large slow workman, who usually sat outside. I used to bottle fruit, mainly plums, and if I could not get the top off the Kilner jar I would take it over and ask him to do it; he had what we called a "cushy number" and it was the only work I saw him do all through the war.

We were issued with gas-masks and wearing them it was not at all easy to breathe, after they added an extra section on the end it was almost impossible.

If my father was home he would go into the country to visit his relatives and shoot rabbits. At one time they were very important to us, we practically averaged eating one rabbit a week, and I do not know what we should have done without them. I remember him shooting crows once, there is not much on a crow one can eat but we made them into a crow pie. We preserved eggs in waterglass (Isinglass, gelatine made from the swim bladders of certain fish) in a large crock in a pantry in the basement, because eggs were difficult to get. Another thing we had was reconstituted (dried) eggs mainly used for cooking and scrambled, which I rather liked. I only ate whale meat once and did not much care for it, it looked like meat but tasted fishy; on one occasion I was served what purported to be beef in a café but there was far too much of it and it had a slightly sweet taste and I suspected that it was horse. Another thing we tried eating wiene nettles but they were not very good they just tasted like boiled chiffon, or how I imagine that would taste. At the beginning of the war we had an allotment up the London Road which largely kept us in vegetables. On one occasion I remember stooking corn at Upcote, something that has completely died out with the advent of combine harvesters. In those days I think there were many more rats about on farms, I remember my father and I watching black rats crawling all over a heap of straw, at the same farm.

The town was full of men from many parts of the world, there were a lot from Poland based at RAF Innsworth. They gave some concerts at the Town Hall, for the first time I heard their male voice choirs accompanied only by sounds they made themselves. It was wonderful and like nothing I had ever heard before, though later it would be made well known by Russian choirs. There were "Free French" and "Free Norwegians" and they all learnt to dance. Soldiers had little to do in their free time, and we had a sergeant who seemed to spend most of his time in our house and go off to mount the guard at Lorriston, a house that had been requisitioned at the top of Montpellier, at 6 o'clock every evening.

One day walking down the street in the snow I saw a tall man in front of me in the uniform of an RAF officer, with a large beard, and a turban on his head - he was the first Sikh I had ever seen. When he reached our house he turned up the steps because of course he was coming to learn to dance. We also had a pupil from Ceylon (Sri Lanka today) who was as black as pitch but spoke English better than I did.

The First Ron

One newcomer to Cheltenham who was to have an important effect on my life was a young man 6'2" tall, from Smiths Industries where he was a tool maker. The factory had been relocated from Cricklewood, London to Cheltenham at the beginning of the war and after a few years, like everyone else he came to dancing classes. He was an apt pupil and soon became my dancing partner. I suppose almost from birth I had been destined for the stage and first appeared at the Town Hall at the age of three. My family were not churchgoers and I knew nothing about the Church, but I did know all about dancing; my grandmother once took me to a wedding, as a toddler, and in a particularly quiet part of the service I said in a loud voice, "I think I'll sit down until they start dancing"!

The training as a ballet dancer became more and more irksome to me, it was hard and uncomfortable and my heart was not in it, also and by the time I was about twelve I had grown too tall to be a ballerina. Training as a ballroom dancer was more agreeable and both Ron and I took to it with ease. We trained relentlessly, some three hours a night to become competition dancers. We became Gloucestershire Champions and then West of England Champions. We used to travel all over the country and I remember being at the Royal Albert Hall on one occasion when my partner had just lined up four whiskies at the bar, one each for us and two of them for my parents, when a heat was announced; he lost his head and not knowing what to do for the best downed all four with the result that he kept doing the same steps, or variations as we called them all the time and we received poor markings!

We must have been mad, I remember being driven to a competition, by my father, to Kingston-on-Thames once on a night so icy that a car on the road in front of us turned completely round, and where the hotel in which we stayed was so cold that my mother and I went to bed wearing fur gloves.

Ron and I used to go to a cinema one evening a week, there were six in the town in those days and one sat in the best seats for 3 shillings and sixpence each.

I was still at school, but as well as the dance training in the evenings I also did the shopping and cooking for the family, I acted as receptionist for the dancing school, and did the speech training.

43

Growing up on the Home Front.

There was also the Red Cross cadets and I belonged to a troop concert where we used to go out in a coach to entertain the troops, and I did two Spanish dances. We had a classical pianist and a boogie-woogie pianist who used to have the piano practically leaping off the ground, while the classical one listened with horror in the wings all but chewing his finger nails.

We had a dramatic woman singer (Pauline Allen) and a tap dancer (Pat Newman). One night we got lost in very thick fog on Staverton Airport and even two guards we came upon had lost what they were guarding. It was on one such an occasion that I drank my first and only glass of "Coke": (Coco Cola).

The Home Guard was composed of young men, old men and men in reserved occupations. Ron was in the Smiths Industries Home Guard, and one of the best shots in the platoon. The Town Clerk produced at least two big pageants during the war, half the town took part and the other half formed the audience. They must have been based on history as members of the Home Guard wore various historical uniforms and we always had dancing parts. Once we were in Regency costumes and another time were flappers of the 1920s doing the Charleston.

Ron was committed to the dancing but his other great interest was old cars. In those days these could be purchased very cheaply and it was not unusual for him to have a different one about every six months. He had a fine old open Bentley, a Lagonda, an Alvis and a rather unusual beast called an Avon. Once coming back from London we ran an MG. into the back of a lorry, pretty well wrecking it right back to the dash board. It was raining and the lorry was standing still, the back light was about the size of half a crown and partly covered with mud, so it was not surprising it happened. I passed out and found myself lying on the side of the road. We were on the hill leading down to Northleach so the local hospital was very near and I was soon in bed there. I was not badly hurt and Ron was not hurt at all. My parents came for us in the morning but I think the car must have been a write-off.

We used to drive to Woolwich to have lessons from Henry Jaques, a famous dancing teacher, who often said "It's not like the time when we used to do the Blues". Sometimes even today if I am walking along the street I say to myself "Swing from the hips" and my aged steps cover more ground and get along a little smoother.

We made frequent visits to the Victoria Rooms in Bristol for competitions and I remember driving back from Bath one night when we pulled into the entrance to Dyrham Park and listened to the nightingales singing. It was normal to take a flask of black coffee to have on the journey home, usually with Gorgonzola cheese sandwiches, it was not popular if offered to companions, but it was easily obtainable and Ron and I enjoyed it.

The dancing years with my partner Ron Dodd

At home we all used to gather for supper about 10 o'clock, when mother's classes were finished. I remember when it was Ron's 21st birthday I made a very special soup containing among other things quite a lot of mushrooms. It was followed by an ornate birthday cake, made by aunt Ida's son at the best patisserie in town - rationing made for strange eating habits.

Once a year we would go off camping, usually into Devon and Somerset. It was something that was new to us and I remember the first time we could not find a camping site. We spent the night in the garden of a kindly vicar, putting up our small tent beside our large Bentley. We learnt to love the south west especially around Selworthy and Porlock.

We spent the greater part of our spare time together, he even washed my hair, and mostly things went on very harmoniously. We did, however, practise our dancing for very long periods and I tended to get blamed if things went wrong so that there were times when it got too much for me; once I slapped his face (this was the sort of thing women did then) and he hit me. I think it was probably more surprise than anything that made me scream several times. My parents were upstairs and came rushing down; my father was very belligerent he went for Ron saying "You struck a woman!" by his standards this was not allowable. He wanted Ron to "go outside with him", the inference being to fight. This came up against the younger man's standards who was unwilling to hit an older man, so there was something of a stalemate. The women tried to pour oil on troubled waters, and eventually things settled down, and I could only find comfort in my dancing partner's arms.

Once when we were at a camp site near Selworthy a policeman came to tell us that Ron's father had died suddenly and next morning we had to drive home.

It was 1952 and I was trying to persuade Ron that we should go to the continent for our holidays, but he was strangely unenthusiastic. I suppose he had been putting off telling me because one evening, like a bolt from the blue, he told me he was emigrating to Canada in two weeks time. In the weekend that was left we went to Allerford and stayed at the house beside the little pack-horse bridge. In those days people did not jump into bed with each other as they do now and doubtless young people today will find it difficult to believe that we had been in love for about eight years but had not slept together. In spite of our long association I just felt scared. I suppose it was the first time for both of us because afterwards he said "Well, if that is all it is I think it is highly overrated"!

So in another week he was gone, saying he would send for me when he was settled. He soon moved from Canada to the United States.

I used to write and send the Motor Sport magazine every month. In due course he had a high-pressure job in a firm that made cars and he ran two dancing schools in Chicago. He was still writing long letters to me twenty-seven years after he left. He returned for the funeral of his mother and then his brother. I remember him walking into the shop one day and standing in the middle of it looking rather uncomfortable and I went up and kissed him. He stayed with me on one or both of these occasions, preferring to sleep on my sofa than to use the accommodation provided by his sister.

I must have known long before this that he had married someone else (a widow with two children). It is strange that I cannot remember when I knew. I was out walking in the town when I met someone who had been one of our competitors in the competition world, and she said "Fancy Ron getting married like that!" It was the first I had heard of it.

In 1986 the Artist Blacksmith Association of North America was organising a conference in Arizona and I was planning to go to it and meet Ron so that we could make a trip to the Grand Canyon. Shortly before we made the booking he died suddenly one night and I did not have the heart to go.

So the first Ron was gone and it had a big effect on me, I can still remember the leaden feeling to which I woke each morning. My one lifeline was my attendance at art school classes and it was there that I met the second Ron. But how did I come to be at the art school? I had wanted to study there from my teens and to go full time; it was the only thing I showed real enthusiasm for, but my parents did not consider art to be a viable way of earning a living and it was frowned upon. However I did go part time, even when I was still at school I went on Saturday mornings and over the years I went to life classes and then started modelling and carving as an aid to improving my puppet making.

The Roel Puppets.

Amina and her puppets

I had started making puppets during the war and as time went on I began to work with Olive Blackham as an assistant. She was an extraordinary woman, while still living in Birmingham (where I believe she worked in a bank) she had begun, with friends, to form a marionette theatre for adults, as an art form. One of her collaborators was George Speaight who specialised in the Juvenile Drama or Model Theatre. (Note. He wrote "The Juvenile Drama" published in 1946.) Marionettes for adults, was something of a revolutionary idea, perhaps rather before its time, but her influence must have been considerable.

She spent many years researching into the nature and construction of the string puppet. In those days it was something simply passed from one showman to another, they kept their secrets to themselves and it formed no part in the work of colleges or art schools. She felt the puppet could move gracefully and have a considerable range of gesture "When it is possible to select and control both the movements of the puppet and the form it shall take, then the puppet becomes a valuable medium for dramatic work".

The repertoire included some of the Noh plays of Japan, Chinese folk plays, the medieval play of Abraham and Isaac from the Chester cycle and contemporary English and American poetic plays as well as farces such a Tchekhov's "The Proposal" and original burlesques and satires. A particularly attractive work was "Lima Beans" by Alfred Kreymborg. There were only two characters, the figures were not as high as some of the puppets, I should think about sixteen inches. The puppet heads were wooden and consisted of a sphere for the lady and a cube for the man. They were almost colourless, her dress was beige, as was his shirt, but his trousers were darker, a reddish brown. The female figure was worked in an unusual way the strings were attached to a pair of gloves worn by the operator and attached to a wooden bar. It enabled very slight gentle movements in the hands of a skilled operator. I can still hear Olive's voice

" *Put a knife here*
place a fork there
marriage is greater than love
give him a large spoon,
give him a small -
you're sure of your man when you dine him.
A cup for his coffee
a saucer for spillings
a plate ringed with roses
to hold his night's fillings -
roses for hearts, ah,
but food for the appetite!
Mammals are happiest home after dark!"

In the summer of 1932 she fitted up a stage and workshop in the old granary at Roel Farm near Guiting Power, on the Cotswolds. From 1933 to 1939 she began to tour for part of the year and gave performances at the Unity Theatre and the New Players Theatre, London. The company was chosen by the British Puppet and Model Theatre Guild to represent English Puppetry at the 1937 Paris Exhibition. The advent of the war forced the closure of the theatre.

Olive moved into Cheltenham, staying with her mother in Wellington Street, and again worked in a bank. She not only taught a group of people, of which I was one, to make puppets but also began to run a summer school for the same purpose. One was held in our studio in Montpellier and then in Guiting Power, where we operated in the village hall, and I was one of the instructors.

Amina and Olive practising

After the war school teachers were needed and emergency training colleges were set up and Olive and I travelled all over the country visiting colleges, usually for a few days at a time. Most of the students had served in the forces and made great audiences eager to take in new ideas and to add their own; the difference to the normal student was very marked. We demonstrated the different forms of puppets: shadow, glove, rod-and-glove, rod and string puppets, i.e. marionettes. The two of us performed plays or poems with each type, moving from one form of staging to another and between each, one of us, would describe the way of making and operating the puppets. It took us a considerable time to set up and one and a half hours to do the lecture demonstration

Together with travelling this was all quite tiring, but in some ways it was the socialising that I found more exhausting. The many little coffee parties where everyone was so pleasant and we had to be equally sociable were sometimes too much, you must meet the students after the show, the staff will meet you too, we will take you to the staff room now before you finish getting ready. The colleges must have been extraordinarily enclosed communities, rather like convents, and I suppose new faces were at a premium. To this day I have sympathy with the Royal Family and their endless round of politely meeting their subjects.

Although the war was over, food was still scarce (rationing did not end until 1954) and there are times when I find I remember the food better than the performances. There was one college when everyone was given an orange for dessert; these were very rare and did not run to anyone who had not contributed a ration book so did not include us. Then there was another college where we had stewed greengages which was unusual, and I remember an extraordinary meal that was composed entirely of eggs, and taken with two tutors in their own home. They kept chickens and I think the first course was hard boiled eggs with mayonnaise, then the main course was cooked eggs in some form or other and the dessert was meringue. Full marks for ingenuity but it was some days before one wanted to see an egg again!

We made our journeys by train with an enormous amount of luggage. There was a very large cabin trunk, another almost as large, several cases and a long bundle of staging. Olive was extraordinarily good at jollying along porters and taxi-drivers. I remember one young man on a station in North Wales who when complimented on his efficiency replied "Yes, I don't know why I'm on the Railways"!

THE
CHILDREN'S MARIONETTES

The Marionette Show that is especially designed for Children. For Parties Everywhere. Halls, Hotels, Private and School Parties, Parks, Fêtes, Toy Department Stores.

Repertoire includes:

Folk Tales; Animal Fables; Plays; Poems; "The Dancing Horses"; and the "Poppet" Series.

The Marionettes are beautifully carved and perform in a gay travelling theatre, which can be erected anywhere on a 9' x 6' floorspace.

Fees are moderate, but necessarily vary according to travelling expenses, etc. Private Parties from 2 gns.; Schools, Hotel parties, etc. from 4 gns.

Please give your requirements and ask for a quotation.

AMINA CHATWIN

"St. Albans," Wellington Street, Cheltenham.

Telephone 5086

Leaflet advertising puppet show

One of Olive's sisters lived in Anglesey and once when we were walking across the fields to the house her husband was heard to say "Here comes Olive to put her layer of chaos on top of ours!". We must have visited them earlier, when the war was on, because I clearly remember Olive standing beside the fireplace, her clean-cut features outlined against the wall as we listened to some momentous news on the radio of General Montgomery's battles in the desert.

Once on the way to Manchester we stopped off for a few days walking in the Lake District. Coming down into Borrowdale Olive slipped and fell. She was in a good deal of pain but we managed to reach the youth hostel and thinking she had just sprained her ankle we continued the journey next day. It was three days later on the return to Cheltenham that it was discovered one of the bones in her ankle was broken.

The Lady, the soldier and the shepherd

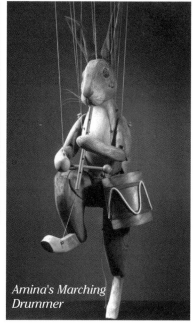

Amina's Marching Drummer

I suppose it is the unusual that stays in the mind, there was plenty of variety, staying in Alnwick Castle, part of which had been taken over for a college, where we slept in a cavernous room with a blazing open fire in the grate; walking round the Mediterranean gardens in the snow at Scarborough, and a deserted funfair area in out of season Ramsgate. Olive had a great zest for life and we never missed the opportunity to walk on the beach or climb the nearest hill. There was an extraordinary college in Ormskirk that was a complete mirror-image of itself. It was perfectly possible to walk miles to the end of the building, thinking one had reached the required room only to find oneself at completely the wrong end of the building.

Olive Blackham

It was the same with exhibitions and museums everything we had time for we visited. In 1945, when we were performing in the London area, we went to the Old Vic to see Laurence Olivier in "Oedipus". It was a wonderful and memorable evening. After the Greek tragedy one felt no desire to see the second part of the programme which was a Sheridan comedy, [The Critic] with Olivier playing Mr Puff. In fact it was extremely enjoyable, altogether perhaps the most memorable evening I have ever spent at a theatre.

We used to do a poem I had written for Glove-and-Rod puppets between a Spanish dancer and a nun-like figure in black. On one occasion we performed it on television at Alexandra Palace.

Olive's puppets were often some two-and-a-half to three feet high and could be very heavy to operate. For a long time she was making figures for Shakespeare's "Tempest" but we only did parts and it never achieved a full performance.

In 1949 Robert Tronson, who later moved to production in television, and Alice Woudhuysen, who was art trained and made some excellent shadow puppets, joined Olive and they made a tour for the Arts Council of Great Britain.

Basically there was never enough work to sustain the theatre and its operators and although Olive was a wonderful artistic director she was not really a business woman. The important aspect to her work was the influence she exerted on education, both through the Summer Schools, where most of the students were teachers, and the lecture-demonstrations. She also wrote two important books "Puppets into Actors" published by Rockcliff in 1948, where she described the different types of puppets, how to make and work marionettes and the staging required for them. Then in 1960 "Shadow Puppets", published by Barrie and Rockcliff, where she explored the shadow puppets of China, Java, Turkey, Greece, and France, then spoke of the ones made by Lotte Reiniger and Helen Binyon at the Bath Academy of Art.

Olive died in Malvern in 2002 aged 103, obituary in The Times July 20th, and left her puppets to The National Puppetry Archive in Bridgnorth, Shropshire. [Amina Chatwin's own puppets and related books are now part of the Archive, Ed.]

I Discover Europe with Ron II.

So after Ron I had gone my life-line was attending classes at the Art School. It was there that I met the second Ron. We peered at each other round the naked bodies of our models in the life class. As I came out of class one evening he was bending over the Vespa scooter he rode and looking up asked if I would like a lift - little did either of us know that it would be round half Europe.

He was an industrial chemist and was about to change his life going to what was then St. Paul's College to train in art to become a teacher of Art and Craft. It was about this time that he began to grow a beard, and when he was sketching in the street one day watched by two small children - one said to the other "He's an artist but he's cut his beard off"! We shared an interest in the puppets and indeed in all art.

Ron II

At the end of his first year at St. Paul's he started to live in one of the rooms over the Montpellier studio and to take his evening meals with us. At the end of the meal my grandfather would take his leave, saying, "Good-night Vin, good-night Phyll, good-night Amina, good-night Ron." The first time he said it to Ron II we all laughed, it came out so pat, after all he had been saying it to Ron I for years!

Ron was talking of going for a trip round Europe on the Vespa scooter and I longed to go but he explained it was not large enough for two with luggage, then suddenly, miraculously, it became a Triumph twin-cylinder motorcycle.

We set off with high hopes; it seemed to take us longer to reach Dover than we anticipated and as it began to grow dark it was raining and coming towards traffic lights we skidded and both came off the motorcycle. I was sliding along the rough tarmac surface of the road, the bulk of Ron's body faintly visible beside me in the darkness and sparks flying upwards as the road ground off the end of one of the handlebars. We must be taught from an early age not to sit in the middle of a dark road; it was instinct that motivated me to the curb, to sit gently swaying forward and back while passers-by asked me where I was hurt. I had lost one shoe, the sock was in ribbons and stained pink with a mixture of rain and blood. Then Ron who seemed to only have suffered a tear in his jacket was helping me to my feet. The impulse that propelled us to Dover was slow to leave its hold over me and I was just beginning to suggest going on when the ambulance arrived. Then I was going back five miles in the wrong direction, to Redhill Hospital. I could not rid my mind of the necessity of catching the boat, but the kindly ambulance man assured me that there would be another boat and we could catch the next one.

There was quite a large cut on my right knee and a smaller one on my left arm. The doctor was sympathetic, he had suffered an accident on a sports holiday in France and warned me how quickly my francs would disappear if I had to buy penicillin there. He took every precaution against sepsis complaining bitterly, as he took pieces of dirt and wool from the wounds, that he was sick and tired of sewing up motorcyclists and would give anything to do a nice clean appendicitis operation.

Sewn up, injected with penicillin and fortified with sandwiches we were finally shown out of the hospital by a sister who made it plain that she considered that it was a foolish and frivolous project to go to France at any time and that if we continued to do so in our present state we should doubtless reap the desserts we deserved.

We had nothing but praise and thankfulness for the skill and kindness with which we had been treated at that hospital; I suppose it was understandable that an establishment that never shut, but functioned night and day alike, should cheerfully eject us into a sleeping town sometime between 1.30 and 2 a.m. with optimistic directions to the nearest hotel. I should think we tried half a dozen all dark and lifeless, only one showed any life and that was full. My leg was beginning to return to life and becoming more painful, obviously we could not ride on. The wooden bench at the police station was hard but the sergeant, serving out strong tea was helpful.

In the early hours of the morning I realised that only eighteen miles away I had good friends at Horsham and we resolved to throw ourselves on their hospitality. If they were surprised at my sudden appearance at breakfast time, heavy-eyed and dishevelled, and accompanied by a man with a large beard that they had never met or even heard of before, they did not show it.

We should not reach Dover for another three days, then Ron decided to go there on the Triumph while I took a train. It was then that I made the discovery that if you limp along covered with bandages you find a great deal of kindness. Porters hurried to help me and refusing tips, took me from one platform to another on the luggage lifts so that I should not have to negotiate steps.

So at last we were on French roads, where people wish you "bon appetit" if you picnic on the verge; where afternoon villages are shuttered and deserted. There are two ways to cross the road in France, if you live on a route national, you grab your companions hand and run as if the devil were after you, or alternatively if you do not live on such a road you spend your time permanently ambling down the middle of it or playing boules across it.

In Paris we stayed at the Hotel Perfect and after the meal at a little café we saw the white domes of Sacré Coeur and drawn towards them ascended the steps, all three hundred of them, for my part one at a time as a child climbs. Next morning we took the Metro to Pont Marie and at some point passed the flower market and saw Notre Dame; then walked along the quays on the Ile de St. Louis, lunching on omelettes at a small café. Madame and the waitress are genuinely friendly and wanted to know how I came to be injured and why my legs are so bruised. We parted more friends than customers. I wonder if French bars are still the same with workmen coming in for their mid-morning coffee and cognac, a small boy sitting on a high stool drinking his wine and water through a straw.

That night we went to the Folie Bergère, arriving on the motorcycle and going the wrong way up a one-way street! Oddly I thought on the whole it was a particularly well dressed show, but one scene that especially appealed to me was an enchanted forest, icy and white with frost, where beautiful women with graceful white bodies carried branches of lighted candles amongst the trees until it began to snow and the white flakes fell gently over all until the scene faded away.

We left Paris by the south for Fontainebleau and had a picnic lunch in the forest, and a fine view of the chateau when we passed it later in the afternoon. By evening as it was beginning to get dark, we arrived at Auxerre where they were celebrating the anniversary of the liberation. We found a cheap but pleasant room in a small friendly hotel with excellent food. In the middle of dinner le patron rushed in and escorted us over the road and into the back of the Town Hall so that we could see the Town brass band marching round in celebration. There was still a great deal of good will and camaraderie remaining between the allies.

Next day it is Sunday and we walk round Auxerre to find a post box and some food for lunch, and see that a lot of both men and women are wearing national costume. We have lunch at the side of a hilly track, where black grapes are growing on each side of the path and see for the first time dark butterflies, much larger than the usual varieties in England.

By evening we arrive in Lyon where we have been told to find the hospital so that the stitches can be taken out of my leg. The Hotel Dieu is a large dark barrack-like looking building. We go through an archway and into a courtyard, where I stretch my French to the utmost to explain my requirements. The rooms are reminiscent of cellars or an old monastery and the doctors wear little square caps and long butcher-like aprons down to their ankles, which no doubt once were white. I notice the hand basins in the corner of the casualty theatre are black with grime, but the doctors are kindly enough and since only one of them has a few words of English, my attention is taken up by making myself understood. They sweep some blood from where I am to lie and the youngest doctor, who speaks a little English, removes the stitches from my leg and arm, a cigarette in his mouth with a long length of ash hovering over the semi-open wound! There is a good deal of head shaking and I keep saying optimistically "C'est bon?" but meet only with shrugged shoulders, not very encouraging. They put a bandage on my leg which falls off before we reach the road. I thank them and say they have been very kind to which one replies that England does not seem to have been very kind to me, we find an hotel right by the back of the hospital.

We were always too tired to make an early getaway; it was already hot and one began to hug the shade. As we journeyed along, the country became much more southern, with patches of sweet-corn, melons and peach orchards.

By the time we reached Orange it was dark and while looking for an hotel we see a British motorcycle and a man unloading it. He is a doctor from Kings Hospital coming up from the south with his wife. They have been long enough from England to enjoy a chat and after we have found an hotel and cleaned up we go back and talk to them. We are able to fix them up with a bolt they need for their motorcycle and he is kind enough to look at my leg.

Orange has almost an eastern feel, narrow streets, little stinking alleys, bead curtains across doorways and outside the greengrocers fantastic mounds of fruits, melons, peppers, and aubergines with which I would be far more familiar now than I was then. We went over the fine Roman theatre before leaving.

Through Aix-en-Provence and see signposts to Marseilles and then Toulon but get hopelessly lost. The country becomes more and more difficult until we begin to go up mountains in a series of hairpin bends always with a precipice on one side; lavender grows wild on the hills and the views are magnificent; but always as one rounds a bend, imagining the top has been reached other peaks appear ahead. Then we seem to aim upwards between two gleaming white outcrops of rocky peaks that rear up against the sky and to the left we see far off our first glimpse of the Mediterranean. Then it is continuously downwards until we reach Fréjus. I sit outside a café and Ron, who seems to have been elated rather than intimidated by the mountains, goes off to find an hotel. We talk to four men on two large English motorcycles.

That evening there is some sort of lizard or scorpion on the ceiling of the dining room but I don't look too closely.

We get to San Raphael and remember we forgot to call at a post office to see if there are any letters. I wait on some rocks, being terribly tired, and Ron rides back to Fréjus, just as well because he finds we have left our passports at the hotel and the post office will not be open until 2 p.m. We have pasties for lunch and sun bathe. There are palm trees all along the front in a great semi-circle along the beach.

We stop at Cannes and walk round the harbour and see the boatmen playing boules on the sands, and continue to Golfe-Juan. Stay at the Hotel Jeanne d'Arc, a beautiful house in a palm avenue. Palm trees in the garden with geraniums growing up the trunks, and mauve bougainvillea climbing over the house. Our room opens on to a balcony and there is a mosquito net over the bed.

It is twilight when we return to the beach so that Ron can bathe, then we have an excellent meal at a verandah restaurant built out over the sea. We throw bread to shoals of little fish, there are soft lights, music, wine and the lights of Juan-les-Pins twinkling over the bay.

We get a fairly early start because we had breakfast on our balcony. The road to Nice is much the same as on the previous day, very twisting up and down with beautiful views over the sea. Coming up the hill above Nice harbour we stop to admire the panoramic view and meet an English couple on another motorcycle. We talk and continue on together, stopping at Monaco and all having a beer together beside a street market.

We lunch at Menton where there are shops with delightful Provencal fabrics, hand printed and all made up into skirts, mats or bags quilted in tiny squares. Soon after Menton we circle upwards and are at Customs, then across the border into Italy. All along the coast the road has been twisting but now we start on continuous Z bends which continue for days. Sometimes the road goes through tunnels cut in the rock and usually one looks down over rocks to the sea, which being seen from above is unbelievably blue.

Now that France is left behind one sees fewer British tourists and begin to have quite a fellow feeling for French holidaymakers, who one often meets on Vespas or small cycles. We even get to the waving stage with two young Frenchmen who crossed the border at the same time we did and buy their petrol coupons when we do.

By evening we reach Alassio and stay at a German owned hotel with enormous cacti in the garden. We see a line of horse drawn carriages waiting for fares. One seems to see this in most Italian towns; the horses wear straw hats often trimmed with flowers and one in Alassio had a fine plume of pheasant feathers up the front. In the country one sees the farm horses wearing cotton headdresses over the neck and forehead usually plain white or striped.

In the morning the owner comes to see us off when we go, and putting his hand on the saddle of the Triumph indicates the bumpy nature of the roads and says "England to Rome, for me, No!" He also informed Ron that with his beard he looks 49 instead of 29.

Genoa was a nightmare, there was so much traffic we were continuously held up at traffic jams. At one time I thought it just is not possible to find a vehicle that is not on this road. There were cars, lorries, trams, bicycles, motorcycles, scooters, everything I thought - but behold a few minutes later a massive steam train appeared, on some rails I had not seen, and actually chugged down the road! We gave up trying to see anything in Genoa and just concentrated on getting though the place. On the outskirts we stopped and I bought bread and some nice almond tarts and Ron got a bottle of Chianti. It is a common thing to see motorcyclists going along with a bottle of Chianti tied on somewhere! We stopped to eat our lunch on the beach just the other side of Genoa, glad to rest in peace for a while. Little children were playing in the sand, even those of about three years old wearing tiny gold rings in their ears. We had hoped to reach La Spezia but the road was so difficult that it was dark by the time we reached Rapallo and we were exhausted.

In the morning we found the beach crowded but Ron had a swim, something I was not allowed because of the wound in my leg. We ate lunch on the top of a pass where we spoke to a Pole from London who was being given a lift by two Florentines from Florence to Milan. We all had quite a conversation, he could speak Italian and acted as interpreter when the Italians asked about the Triumph, in which they seemed very interested. The Pole gave us the address of a café where we could eat cheaply in Florence and we all parted with mutual good wishes for our journeys.

I think it was this day that we began to see the little hilltop villages built on the pinnacles of the hills. The road descends from the 2,000ft pass and brings one down to the coast at La Spezia. At a level crossing we met an Englishman on a motorcycle who more or less kept with us and we looked at Pisa together. He was travelling alone and I think was glad of someone to talk to. At another such stop we met four American girls in a terribly tumble-down little car with luggage strapped all over it. They were in great spirits and had been over the best part of Europe, though how such cars stick together on these trips is a mystery to me.

Around Carrara one sees great slabs of quarried marble at the sides of the road and in stonemasons' yards and on one occasion I caught a glimpse of a craftsman in a small dark workshop working at a white marble carving that looked like a piece of frieze or moulding.

One sees Pisa across the plain, away to the front right of the road, all laid out so neatly that even at this first glimpse of the tower and the Basilica it can all be made out clearly. Oddly, one hardly needs to go to Pisa, because it is so exactly what is expected from photographs, so white, so exact, and the tower leaning just as you know it will.

Following the coast beyond Pisa the road seems flatter and lower than the previous coastal stretches, night was beginning to fall and we saw dark rocks jutting out into the sea and after trying several places to stay, we at last found an hotel at Castiglioncello. After tea we walked in the direction of the sea because we hoped to see a romantic moonlit stretch of the Ligurian Sea but we found only some rather smelly back streets!

Next day towards late afternoon we sighted the walled hill town of Tarquinia, high above us. We turned from the main road towards the ancient Etruscan city. The hill on which it stands rises sharply from the plain and the road takes you straight to the main square.

Being Sunday evening everyone was assembled there and a large foreign motorcycle ridden by a bearded man and a girl in shorts, and both wearing crash helmets, which were then almost unknown in Italy, created an excessive stir. I had never been so much stared at before. We went into the Palazzo Vecchio, now the museum, as it was almost time for it to close. It is a most beautiful Renaissance building and one enters through tremendous doors into a square open courtyard, round which there are Etruscan stone coffins. Various dark stone rooms contain sarcophagi of noble Etruscan families with sculptures of reclining nobles far more impressive than any photographs I had seen of Etruscan work. Returning to the courtyard, a broad flight of wide, shallow and beautifully proportioned steps circle upwards to the galleries above. Here one can look downwards into the courtyard or over the old red tiles of surrounding roofs and across the plain to the distant sea. We should like to have lingered but the museum was being shut and we had to hurry down the stairs, not that it was possible to hurry down stairs that seem made for the slow and gracious steps of Renaissance nobles.

Outside, the square was still thronged with people but determined to see what we can of the town we brave the stares of the inhabitants and walk along one of the main streets, which seems to be used as a kind of promenade. Whole families out for their Sunday evening stroll stare intently as they come towards us and we found that if we stopped and looked behind us, or cast sidelong glances over our shoulders, there they would all be, stopped and turned round to stare when they had passed us by! One young boy found it most difficult to walk along in front of us and push a bicycle with his head turned permanently backwards to inspect us. In the street which goes straight from the main entrance of the town there were quantities of people, mostly men, listening to voices over a loud speaker, political or sporting I did not know which, but I am sure it was nothing to the entertainment we afforded that night. While we put on our helmets, mounted the motorbike and wheeled it out of the square we were duly and solemnly watched by every single person present - I felt like waving and saying "Hope you enjoyed the show"!

We had a bit of trouble in Rome looking for somewhere to stay. A foxy little waiter, speaking streams of Italian, battened on to us in a very dodgy neighbourhood. His movements were made at an incredible speed surpassed only by the rate at which words came out of his mouth. He seemed determined to find us somewhere to stay. We refused to leave our belongings or the motorcycle; but did briefly enter a grim and filthy tenement he led us to. We finally made our getaway pressing a few lire into his hand to get rid of him. His peculiar brand of helpfulness persisted even to the end, as he wrote "Grand Hotel" and an address on a piece of paper. As we departed, his voice still ringing in our ears, it perhaps speaks well for his character that I think his words were directions and not curses!

Amina with the bike

We pulled up in some gutter and ready to clutch at any straw and started looking for a railway station on the assumption that there ought to be hotels or lodging houses nearby; it was then that an English voice fell on our ears and the voice of the ancient gods themselves could not have been more welcome. An Englishman and an Irishman directed us, in words we could understand to a Catholic hotel that sounded like paradise. It felt like it too as I fell asleep that night, for at Casa Pallotti we met with not only comfort but also with kindness, the receptionist even leading us along the streets himself, to a little basement café where we could obtain a meal, in case we should not find it for ourselves.

Next day we set off to see Rome on foot. Later I should spend much longer times in Rome, once for three weeks I concentrated on looking at early church mosaics. This first time, which must have been about two days, we went to St. Peters and the wonderful Bernini colonnade, the Castel Sant' Angelo and next day the Coliseum and the Forum.

Originally we had intended to continue to Naples and Pompeii but our accident at the beginning had meant it was necessary to go no further south than Rome. So now we headed northwards to Arezzo where there was a street procession which seemed to be something to do with celebrating Hannibal. The Italians always have such exciting processions with great big flags and people wearing medieval costume.

We went to Florence looking down on it first from a viewing point on the road. We found the place to eat we had been recommended and went round the cathedral [The Duomo] and the Uffizi gallery. I had some romantic notion of looking at Florence by moonlight but Ron was in a very bad temper, perhaps I was not the right woman, and in the end he went out by himself and said there was nothing to see. Some while before I met Ron he had been about to get married, but his best man went off with the bride-to-be practically on the eve of the wedding - I think in those days I did not realise how physiologically traumatised he had been by the experience.

Next day Florence was a little restored to me when I bought just what one ought to buy in Florence a pair of large filigree and pearl earrings. Next day crossing the Apennines in beautiful country we descended down the foothills. Just as we rounded a Z bend, a bee flew into the side of Ron's helmet and stung his face. We said what a good job we did not fall off, yet a few minutes later and a few yards later, as we rounded the very next bend, the machine slipped on some loose gravel on the side of the road and we did fall off! This time I was fortunate because Ron landed underneath, but neither of us was much damaged, but the Triumph was indeed a sorry sight, the headlamp glass was smashed, the whole front twisted round and the fork suspension jammed. There was a solitary café a few yards down on the other side of the road and a man and a woman were eating at a table outside. The man came rushing to pick us up and brush us down, and when we had cleaned up the odd scratches he helped us to manhandle the bike to rights. He asked us if we were headed for Bologna and we nodded "Yes to Venetezia", his eyebrows shot up and we took his best wishes with us! Soon after there was Bologna with the two so well known leaning towers thrusting upwards from the middle of the town. We found a restaurant and later Ron said I must have been in a bad state because it was the only time of the whole trip that I walked in without first ascertaining the price. Well, if we had known the price we should not have walked in, but how much we enjoyed the lasagne, the first I had ever tasted, the stuffed gherkins and tomatoes, and the veal cutlets topped with thickly sliced ham and melted parmesan cheese. By the time we reached the sweet we were getting worried about the lire and I never tasted the slices of cake soaked in liqueur and topped with buttered almonds and whipped cream.

So we came to Venice across the causeway from Mestra. Later I should come to know and love Venice; it would be forty years before I returned again and it is difficult to remember what we saw that first time. I feel we rode in at night because I remember the lights reflected in the water and Place de Roma was just an extension of the main land, surely it was covered with stalls of melons, silk squares and scarves tied in great bunches, postcards and trinkets and necklaces of gleaming mother-of-pearl and string upon string of spiky red coral. I have never ceased to be delighted by the necklaces they sell in Venice. I remember how much we enjoyed the narrow streets, the tiny dark shops where craftsmen worked on carved and gilded furniture.

I do not remember at all where we stayed that first night, on the mainland I think, but I remember sitting beside a canal next day for coffee and watching the late arrival of daily deliveries of grain, crates of bottles of aqua mineral. A little boy jumped from a barge and balancing precariously worked his way along a café railing to deliver a bundle of newspapers. The coffee finished, a bright-eyed little boy asked for the packets of sugar that were left and scuttled away with a packet for himself and one for his friend as pleased as if he had found a treasure.

We rode in a vaporetto, it is something I never tire of doing, to glide along past the varied architecture of the buildings; that first time we saw a gondola propelled by two men in white liveries embellished with red and gold sashes and we passed, for the first time, under the Rialto Bridge. It must have taken us some time to make our way through the narrow streets of shops full of gorgeous merchandise until we turned through some arches and suddenly there was the Square of San Marco stretching before us. It was enormous and it was covered with people and hundreds of pigeons. The facade of San Marco is staggering, the coloured mosaics in the arches above the doors, the four magnificent bronze horses that stride onwards as if they would walk across the Square. The way the whole gleams with gold and speaks of the east, as far removed from the Gothic cathedrals that I have been brought up with as it is possible to be.

In Vicenza we stopped almost outside the Palladian theatre. I had hoped so much to see it and time was made and I never regretted it, it is one of the most beautiful buildings I have ever seen. The elaborate proscenium facade with the false prospective streets leading out of it - the steep tiers of stone seats with the columns and statues above, culminating in the cloudy painted sky of the ceiling.

It was imperative that we press on; we stopped at a café for coffee and as we left I was amused to see a man with his two sons mount a small motorcycle, all three one behind the other, the smallest perched in the middle. As it grew dusk it became one of the worst evenings riding I can remember. No cyclist in Italy, at any rate in the country, dreams of having a light, and driving the motorcycle in the half-light with cyclists, carts and led oxen literally all over the road was nerve-racking in the extreme. Our lights were poor too and at one point we drove straight off the road on to an unmade lane with Ron still protesting that he could see perfectly well. The nocturnal journey seemed interminable and we went through a dim archway in one village, failed to see that the road bent around to the right, amended the course by passing, on the wrong side, in front of a lorry. The road was darker and bumpier all the time and with my nerves in shreds, one particularly pulverising bump reduced me to tears. My morale rebuilt by Ron's unfailing kindness we pressed on - until we ran out of petrol! We trudged along the road, surprisingly I felt better, perhaps it was relief at being once more on my own two feet. Some Italians in a car kindly stopped and asked if they could help but we had nothing in which to put any petrol. Then we remembered the little can of petrol we used for our stove; this we emptied into the tank and the Italians followed along behind us until we reached the next garage. It was typical of the kindness we met with on the whole trip. We were aiming for Como but decided when we arrived at Lecco to stay there as we had both had enough for that evening.

In the early hours of the morning we were awakened by someone trying to unlock the door of our room. Sometimes the endless roads of the daytime became part of my sleep and as I began to wake I said "it goes downhill", Ron, never at a loss, merely agreed with me and as I woke fully and said "it's someone trying to get in", I could feel him tense beside me ready to jump up and tackle any intruder. It was strangely disturbing there in the dark with the foreign voices outside in the corridor. It seemed to go on for ages and I felt it could only be smugglers or men about some nefarious practice, it was a long time before I settled down relaxed enough to sleep.

At Lake Como we saw a buddleia tree covered in the most beautiful butterflies including one large yellow swallowtail, that I had never seen before. We passed Lake Maggiore and crossed the Simplon Pass into Switzerland, so clean and fresh, houses with overhanging eaves, shutters and flowers everywhere, Lausanne, Berne and Interlaken.

We were really having to travel now, there was less time for sightseeing, and catching the boat loomed large.

We came towards Zurich late one night and saw all the lights spread out along the river Limmat. Through Schaffhausen and the Black Forest, high and cold, to Friberg. We fear we shall not reach the boat in time and try to get on a train at Metz without success, so we press on to Luxembourg, then Brussels and finally Dunkirk.

To Madrid in [1956]: the Second Journey.

The following year we rode down to Madrid and back. We stopped at Bayeux to see the tapestry. I remember some ancient houses, the faded beams, the overhanging upper storey criss-crossed with a herringbone of timbers, and the carving of a Madonna upheld by a bracket.

On the way south we went to two chateaux and I cannot even remember which ones they were. We were anxious to see some of the caves with Palaeolithic paintings and were heading for the Dordogne. We were very happy at the Soleil d'or in Montignac, where we had a charming room in the annex that had a brass bedstead and the walls papered with pink roses. It had a French window with grey shutters and a straight narrow paved path into the garden. When we enquired if we could have a bath they said of course only the water system had broken down but the patron would send across a jug of hot water. When a boy came he bore two of the largest jugs of the hottest water I had ever seen and there was no need for either of us to go dirty that night.

In the morning it was market day and stalls were set up in the main street. Every man in the place wore a beret, never even in the Basque country, have I seen such a varied and complete collection. They topped every male head in the village, tall men and fat men, red faced or pale, small berets like pimples, large ones like omelettes drooping about the ears. Men stood in groups wearing them while driving cows down the street. They sold vegetables in the gutter or strolled opulently along the pavement displaying gold watch chains across well-rounded waistcoats to offset the noble and jet-black felts upon their heads.

The Dordogne country is beautiful in the extreme and we were very happy riding along - counting magpies one for sorrow two for joy, three for a girl, four for a boy.

We went first to Font-de-Gaume from Les Eyzies; there was a rough area of grass outside the entrance to the cave, where an old lady tended an iron pot on a tripod over a fire. There was a system of electricity for the cave but it had failed and we were shown round by an elderly lady holding a lamp. It showed the paintings infinitely better than any I should ever see lit by electricity. The cavern is a corridor 120m long with three secondary corridors leading from it. The first paintings are 65m from the entrance, which making ones way slowly along in the semi-dark seems quite a distance, wild cattle, horses, reindeer, and mammoth are all here. Both Font-de-Gaume and les Combarelles were discovered in 1901 by Henri Breuil, Louis Capitan and D. Peyrony within a week of each other. The old sinter deposits that covered the engravings at Combarelles and the paintings at Font-de-Gaume dispelled any doubts there might originally have been about their belonging to the Ice Age. The art at both Font-de-Gaume and Combarelles was copied by the Abbé Breuil so that one cannot help but be influenced by his work, especially as the original paintings are tending to fade.

However, I have always thought that the extreme sensitivity of many Ice-Age paintings completely dispels any idea that Palaeolithic man was in any way less perceptive than we are today. These are not the work of brutish or primitive peoples.

A kilometre or more away from Font de Gaume towards Sarlat the cavern of Combarelles lies off the D48. In many ways it is less impressive than the former because the art is engraved not painted, and many of the engravings are superimposed one on top of another, which makes them difficult to see. It seems to me the cave was often narrow and I think it may have been that one had to go through a part that was very low, so that there was an uncomfortable feeling becoming suddenly almost aware of the great weight of earth above.

Moving south, we saw the fortified bridge at Cahors. We crossed the Pyrenees loud with the sound of bells from sheep and goats. We travelled from the frontier post at Canfranc towards Madrid. There were many ruins of buildings and villages still remaining from the Spanish Civil War. It is an unyielding land of barren sun-baked stones, each plain bounded only by the next range of mountains and yet another plain and more mountains. A land of dried up river beds glinting in the sun, where men work the soil and thresh the harvest as they must have done since biblical times. Outside the main towns of this area motor traffic seemed almost unknown.

Looking back on this journey I can see that the great advantage of travelling on a motorcycle is that one is with the people and accessible to those on the road in a way completely different to being shut away in a car. In a remote part we came to a group of workman making up a road, an extraordinarily rough and stony road; I do not recall if we were going very slowly or pushing the vehicle, but they included us in their group conversation and showed us what they were talking about and gesticulating over - a locust. Well it is the only one I have ever seen and judging by their interest and enthusiasm it must have been a rarity also to them. Note: Locusts are usually found in North Africa and Asia.

We had coffee or lunch one day sitting outside at a table by the great Roman aqueduct of massive stones at Segovia.

Avila was a town of beggars who ruined the place for us. We probably made the mistake of giving a coin to a gypsy woman early on and were pursued relentlessly by them, keeping up a high pitched whining for alms. Finally I lost my patience and spat out "No Nada!", it seemed to do the trick.

My mother was staying with friends in Madrid and we joined them in the flat in General Mola, One could look down to a little pottery below where all the jars were laid out in rows drying in the sun. We enjoyed the Rastro market where one could buy woven blankets and saddle bags and second-hand things of all kinds.

Somewhere in Spain, I cannot remember if it was going south or travelling back up north, we came to a town where General Franco was making a speech from a balcony. I have no idea what he said, but he certainly ended by crying out "Ariba, ariba, ariba!" and the crowd bayed its approval. I knew exactly what this meant because our friends had a small son at the crawling stage and everyone shouted "Ariba" at him - "get up, stand up!".

On the return journey we went straight up to Burgos and its cathedral, then to the cave of Altimira nineteen miles from Santander.

The paintings at Altimira were first noticed in 1875 but not appreciated until four years later when Sanz de Sautuola, a local gentleman and landowner, whose interest had already been aroused by Palaeolithic art, recognised them for what they were. The tale is well known how, when he was digging in the cave for early tools in 1879, the paintings were seen by his little daughter who cried "Look Papa oxen". It took some years for a sceptical world to accept them as genuine. The paintings are mostly of bison and only some thirty yards from the entrance. The height of the cave is in some parts no more than six or seven feet and in the centre there seemed to be a build-up of rocks or earth so that one had to almost lean back on it to see the paintings on the ceiling. They are magnificent animals, some more than 2m in length.

It was probably late afternoon when we arrived at Lascaux, in the Dordogne. They only allowed a certain number of people into the cave each day and as we waited on a broad staircase leading down into the cave one noticed that it became increasingly difficult to breathe. It was the fear that the dampness of peoples breath could affect the paintings that caused it to be closed not long afterwards. We were fortunate to see it then for it is the most important and best preserved of all the caves.

The cave was only discovered in 1940 and the paintings were extraordinarily vivid. A great cavern, known as "The Hall of Bulls", 33 yards in length, opens before one; a mythical spotted and horned animal on the left and over all gigantic black-outline bulls interspersed with horses, auroch cows and goats. There is a stag with a magnificent spread of antlers, a line of rather chubby ponies and a frieze known as swimming deer, and it certainly looks as if they are depicted swimming a river. The largest of the animals, the bulls, are each up to eighteen feet in length.

Amina

Palaeolithic painting would become a lasting interest in my life. As usual we began to get short of time as we headed home; we had had a wonderful time together. I daresay Ron had been putting off telling me, because we were on the ferry crossing the channel when he told me that he had decided to marry one of his students.

I Go and Work in Paris, 1957-58

I think I cried practically non-stop for six months. I realised that desperate situations require desperate remedies, and I answered an advertisement for a job in Paris, in The Lady magazine. I went to London for an interview; in those days I would have taken the train and if my memory serves me correctly the return fare was 27/6 on the Cheltenham Flyer which took very little time. The job was cook/housekeeper to the British Military Attaché and his family. They would not be leaving for Paris for a while and still had other people to interview. I arranged to take a Sorbonne language course at the Cité Universitaire.

I left England at the end of July 1957, my dear father saw me off and we were both holding back tears. Beside us there was an elderly lady saying goodbye to a clergyman; once the train started she could see I was shedding a few tears and was very kind to me. She suggested I sat in her carriage and talking to her I felt better.

I enjoyed my stay at the University city, everything there was very new to me. I found the classes difficult as everything was conducted in French and the odd word of English would have been so much help. After a few days I settled into a class which included Noelle, an Irish girl who would become a lasting friend to me, one other English girl, five Americans, three Spaniards, an Italian man, one Turk, one Japanese and one German girl. I had taken a little camping stove heated by meths and found it to be extremely useful, people could come into my room and have a cup of coffee with me; sometimes they even borrowed it to have friends to their own room, and then contributed a little meths.

It was not only the classes that were cosmopolitan, in the evenings most of us would end up eating at Chapelaines a small café with long narrow tables and a clientele from all over the world. One could eat well there and cheaply; it was there I met an American Marine that I went out with several times, he was scared of French women and I was scared of French men, so we formed a kind of mutual protection society. Here also, Frederick Ludwig M.D PhD would be found most evenings, a German who worked at the Atomic Research Centre outside Paris.

His mother had been killed in an English air-raid during the war. He took me out to coffee on the Montparnasse Boulevard on his Lambretta. His conversation ranged widely over psychology, philosophy, John Stuart

Mill, the colour problem, comparisons of countries and people in general and was likely to suddenly say "Whom do you consider the greatest English mathematician?" Well it kept me on my toes and there was never a dull moment.

After the course finished at the Cité Universitaire I went to Fontainebleau to a family who were with N.A.T.O, to go with them to Caldetas near Barcelona. There I was to look after their two children and two others from the family of the Norwegian consul to Barcelona who were going to join us there. We travelled south in a large Chevrolet that rocked in every direction and I was only saved from sickness by the youngest child who wanted to "fly" his aeroplane out of the window which let in some welcome fresh air. We covered some 345 miles the first day taking us to Cahors and its ancient bridge. It was here in the evening that we had omelettes flavoured with truffles it was the first and only time I have ever tasted them. They were a delicate and unusual flavour but I felt did not hold a candle to a good English wild field mushroom.

Caldetas was a charming little place on the coast a few miles north of Barcelona. It was getting quite a lot of new houses but it was still unspoilt. Above a wooded hill there was an 18th century Martello tower and below were terraced gardens between the houses, with groves of aloes and bamboos between them. The others tended to take the children down to the beach in the mornings while I tidied up and cooked lunch. I managed to swim most days going down to the beach on my own for a while. Then in the late afternoon I would usually take the children down to play on the beach, before getting them ready for bed.

One day there was a fiesta and I took the children down to it, dressed in their best clean cottons. We went round the stalls, selling toys, earrings, and fans, we watched men playing boules and a monkey and a stall with water tortoises. One could have a photograph taken by an ancient camera with a kind of black sleeve for the cameraman to get underneath. There was a backcloth with a man and a woman dancing, with holes for the heads in which you could stick your face to have your photograph taken, or you could sit on a cardboard donkey for it. Then we sat on a long bench and ate doughnut rings that a man was frying in deep oil and they were delicious. Then we bought a packet of sugared almonds and played on the beach for a while. A twelve-piece band, mostly woodwind and brass, played the most fascinating Spanish music, and everyone made long circles under the trees and danced, always the same dance, hands linked and held high up; starting slowly with a simple behind side, front of steps, It gradually became more lively with pointing one toe and then the other toe and hopping about but always almost on the same spot. We did not get home until 8 p.m. after their usual bed time and even the smallest one walked all the way up the hill without complaint.

I had an elegant pale green praying mantis insect in the kitchen one day, something I had never seen before, or since for that matter. The kitchen was very small and I wrote a letter home describing chaos in it one evening. There was a little oil burner that was very difficult to light but belched forth fire and flame with great gusto. I was trying to heat soup on it and it was emitting vast clouds of black smoke, two of the others were mopping up water from the floor because the icebox leaked and the support had broken and deposited ice and all the contents of the refrigerator on the ground. Someone else was trying to open a large tin of tuna fish with an ancient and inefficient tin opener - it was absolute bedlam. Sometimes flames from the oil burner would leap a couple of feet into the air the soup finally boiled over and straight away put the stove out! After supper we would sit on the verandah with the lights of the little town sparkling below. Mostly we drank white wine of the district, enormous bottles with basket work around them, the five adults drank a four litre bottle in two days but as it cost the equivalent of between 4/- and 5/- nobody cared.

When we returned to Fontainebleau my future employers were not quite ready for me; the Colonel was still in Paris looking for a suitable flat. It was arranged that I should spend two or three weeks at Neuilly, working for a friend of the attaché's wife, whose husband was, I believe, head of MI6, putting her wardrobe in order, shortening, lengthening, fitting, or as she described it "putting her on the map".

The house to which I went was served below stairs, by a cook and a young maid. There was also an elderly man who came in to do the 'rough' work, cleaning, washing etc, which seemed to be the general practise in Paris. I passed the information home in case my grandfather was contemplating a new job! The maid was from the Dordogne and was working in Paris while her fiancé did his National Service. Yvonne, the cook, had been engaged to marry an Italian opera singer who was killed in World War II. I had a graphic description from her of the Duke and Duchess of Windsor when they dined at the house. Mrs P had later dined with the Duchess at their town house where the meal was served off the famous Meissen porcelain, and she could see the Duke cutting down trees in the garden, for both of them were enthusiastic gardeners. My future employers had also dined with the Duke and Duchess but that was at their Mill house in the country, each course on a different set of superb china, the soup being served in small covered individual dishes shaped like little cabbages.

As December 1957 approached we were busy getting the flat in 40 Rue Spontini ready for occupation; making the little gilt chairs and the curves of the Louis XV fauteuil in the salon look a little more English by the judicious placing of occasional ornaments and cushions.

Above the prestigious flats the two top floors were mostly single rooms serving the staff of the families below. My room was two flights up and at first sight did not look too promising. However, I scrubbed and stained the wooden floor, and turned the narrow iron bedstead to the short side of the room where it just fitted. I made a shelf down one side to put books on and fixed a woven raffia mat around the wall, this camouflaged the bed very neatly. I bought some dark red hessian to make a bed cover and Mrs F lent me a beautiful hand woven long Greek cushion to put at one end. I also purchased a cane chair with iron legs, and a large gallon bottle of beautiful pale green glass to make a lamp, and for about 2/6 a yellow "coolie" shade, to stand on the table. So the whole room looked quite modern and pleasant.

My day started early as the Colonel used to ride before breakfast with the French officers, and I would go down to the bakery next door to buy long hot crusty loaves of bread to go with his early morning coffee.

For the first three months I expected daily to get the sack because if I managed to cook the food correctly I failed to serve it in the right dishes. But things gradually improved, there was the glorious day when a French prince said to the Colonel "Where did you find your excellent French chef? and he replied "It is an English lady!".

The Colonel sometimes used to go to shooting parties in the country and return with a brace of pheasants. The first time I was horrified, I had never plucked a bird in my life. I made the effort but it took me most of the day because the feathers were so beautiful. Then someone told me that if I took them to the butchers with a little pourboire they would do it for me.

There was one weekend when the Colonel had gone stag hunting in the Forest of Rambouillet in an outfit that included white breeches and top hat, all very English. I used to make him a little packet of sandwiches to take with him, and he later described how he had just taken them out and was sitting on his horse with the sandwiches in one hand, reins and crop in the other when a French nobleman came past and raised his hat, leaving the Colonel in the embarrassing position of having no hand with which to raise his top hat!

The Colonel was in the Coldstream Guards and there was always much soul searching if they were going on parade or in a procession if the weather was unsettled. Apparently rain can damage the red coats they wear and he had to decide if they ought to have their grey top coat to protect or not.

I have been asked what a military attaché does. He is the liaison between the Ambassador and the military. Quite a lot of the work seems to be of a social nature.

We did a good deal of entertaining, cocktail parties and dinners. I had rather a simple soft black wool dress with short sleeves and a cowl neck, and I wore it to pass round cocktail savouries. Once we had two parties, one on Tuesday and one on Thursday, when I made cocktail savouries for 100 people. I wrote home that this was very successful; I scored a notable success with Col. L who at first used to look at me with a drop-dead expression, when I offered him something to eat and never took anything - but he began to say "Here comes the temptress" and ate all the evening. Brigadier S ate six shrimp savouries one after the other and an Admiral ate ham ones all the evening until he finally tore himself away from them and took a smoked salmon one. We had one man there who commanded the whole of the Republican Guard and an American General too, and of course French Counts and Barons were thick underfoot.

On one occasion Col. and Mrs F joined forces with Brigadier J and his wife inviting some fifty or sixty people. I was augmented by the concierge to take the coats outside, a maitre d'hotel and waiters were brought to serve the drinks and a maid and chef of Brigadier J's. The chef did all the cooking and he and the maid were very jolly so we had an amusing evening in the kitchen, often joined by a very pleasant Welsh driver. The chef wore his tall hat only when Mrs J was in the kitchen. This he managed to achieve because she had a fairly loud voice and he used to hear her coming. She had been told that it was absolutely essential to have two people cooking in the kitchen throughout the party, in actual fact we did not find this necessary and once it had begun we sat down and started drinking champagne. I decided I did not know how to look after myself, French servants never want for anything and the first glasses of champagne poured out were for the chef and myself as a matter of course!

It was while I was at the Cité Universitaire that I met Noelle from Ireland and she had met Othman, a cartographer from Tunisia. At first she found his attentions rather overpowering and he had to understand that we did not behave like this. We had never met an Arab before and were rather intimidated, we feared we might be taken off to the kasbah! She would not go out with him alone, so for months we made up a threesome until she lost her fear and fell in love. Dear Othman, for years I used to send him news of Noelle and he used to send me a wooden box of dates every Christmas. Years later when Noelle returned to Tunisia, she went to his office only to learn he had died a few months earlier.

So it was that the three of us had many happy hours together in Paris, we would go for drinks of an evening and later we took to going to films in the little 'flea-pit' cinemas. Sometimes we walked in the parks or through the streets in the evening amongst the lights. On May day when the women came in from the country to sell little bunches of lily-of-the-valley we went to St. Cloud and picnicked beside the river. Pretty well throughout the time I was there I would continue to see them.

Almost from the beginning I had informal supper parties in my little room. It would just about accommodate six people and the first party I had welcomed friends from six countries, France, Germany, Ireland, Tunisia, Italy and England. It was a squash but a success. I made the coffee on my little camping stove; I no longer remember what we ate but there was plenty of wine, and we certainly did not go hungry or thirsty.

My room looked out on to a yard far below with French windows all round except on one side. The rooms where people lived were like warrens, the windows friendly with inhabitants leaning out of them talking to the people on the other side. On one occasion I wrote home:

"Just now I heard a cat mewing so I looked out and so did a woman from the story above. I said "A little cat?" and she, who could see it, said "Yes" it was crying because it could not catch the birds, then a man's

voice joined in from the window above mine and they both started saying "Malheur" to the cat. It's a very descriptive word and means "sorrow" or "Oh dear" sort of thing. At New Year I saw three people at one window with golden paper crowns on their heads, and the windows opposite are quite picturesque because the inhabitants hang everything outside them, clothes, salads, wine and vegetables. The birds come and sit on the window sills, it is really quite lively up here."

As Christmas approached I was feeling rather depressed when Noelle contacted me to say she had a cold and could I accompany a friend of hers to a tea party given by the Minister of a Scottish church in Paris. I did not have high hopes of it as an entertainment but how wrong I was! I was welcomed like an old friend, The apartment was beautiful, rooms with great mirrors over the fireplaces, comfortable English armchairs and settees, soft lamp light and great vases of gladioli. I talked for a while to a man from Persia and a girl from America, and as the evening progressed many people arrived and we were offered a wonderful array of food. Our host the Reverend Dr Donald Caskie was a kindly grey haired man who had written a book called "The Tartan Pimpernel". Apparently during the war he stayed in France and organised an escape route to Spain and was responsible for getting hundreds of British soldiers and airmen out of France and into Spain. He was captured and tortured by the Gestapo and sentenced to death, either escaping or being reprieved at the eleventh hour, I am no longer sure which. I was greatly impressed by his goodness and great hospitality. I was there again at Christmas when we all sang carols.

If my employers were away for a few days as sometimes happened I had the opportunity to go and do some research on 18th century dancing at the Bibliotheque de l'Opéra. I always remember one evening looking up at the domes of the Opéra as heavy snowflakes fell around them. It is something that has always remained in my mind, as did the beauty of the first spring green leaves on the trees on the "prow" of the île de la Cité.

I noticed many things that I found unusual, even bizarre, two priests on a Vespa wearing all black robes and crash helmets, two nuns on motorised bicycles, a small dachshund wearing a white sweater with a polo neck, a man at a puppet show sharing an ice-cream cornet with a poodle lick and lick about!

As things began to settle down I was sent for a course at the Cordon Bleu, which was especially useful in teaching me the presentation of food. People came and went, once Lord and Lady M from Ireland visited for a few days. Paris in the spring rather went to Lady M's head and she purchased a new hat it was the shape of a top hat but made of gold lame with a large bunch of grapes down one side.

I found the city full of great contrasts of riches and poverty. I saw a street in Montparnasse with prostitutes lining the walls, literally shoulder to shoulder. I grew used to seeing single destitutes lying asleep in the gutter or on the banks of the Seine, but on my way home from visiting a friend from Cheltenham who was living in a very rough neighbourhood, I saw a tragic and haunting sight. It was just beginning to grow dark and was bitterly cold and where the narrow street I was in opened out into a square, I saw a whole group of destitutes huddling together, sitting, caps pulled over their eyes, coat collars turned up against the wind or lying sleeping on the pavement, the dark anonymous 'pauvres' such as one sees in Picasso's early paintings, but I did not realise these conditions still existed and I found it very disturbing to think of these people asleep on the pavements or lying in the gutters all night. Sometimes I see blind beggars and old women singing in cracked voices on street corners; it made me thankful for England and its welfare state. I was able to understand how my grandfather Elston was more or less a socialist because it was these sorts of conditions in England in Edwardian times that shaped his opinions.

In my time off I often went to art exhibitions and in the spring I began to send home a series of letters to my local paper "The Cheltenham Chronicle and Graphic" about the things I did and what was happening in the city.

Politically things were becoming very difficult; in February there was something of a crisis between France and Tunisia. So far as I could make out it started because the governor of Tunisia walked out of talks because he did not like Pflimlin who was forming a government in France, then the French bombed a village in Tunisia saying that it was harbouring Algerian rebels. I was seriously warned not to get caught up in any riots. This was not easy, one evening when I had intended to take a walk along by the river I found the Palais Royal Square packed with people and all road junctions around, from the Louvre to Châtelet, covered with policemen, and traffic stopped for miles.

On the 1st of May, when women come in from the country with little bunches of lily-of-the-valley to sell, Noelle, Othman and I went to St. Cloud to picnic by the river, it was spring in Paris and we all felt light hearted but by the 29th it was as if a light had gone out. Political problems with Tunisia were growing extreme with Tunisians trying to starve out French garrisons. Othman, who came and went fairly frequently, was having trouble getting rooms at the Cité Universitaire after he gave his nationality. There were transport strikes, I suspected censorship and things seemed to be going from bad to worse.

It seemed to be partly to do with General de Gaulle. It transpired that one of the ladies who had been a guest at one of my employer's supper parties had spent a night in jail for sticking up Gaullist posters on walls. De Gaulle was an extremely difficult man and it was said that Churchill had found him so awkward to deal with during the war that he used to say that the greatest cross he had to bear was the Cross of Lorraine - meaning de Gaulle.

By the end of May I was afraid that if the government failed to agree on changes in the constitution this would be the moment for the Gaullists to make a bid for power: the last thing the people of France wanted was violence but those in Algeria did not seem so restrained. It was a real impasse, students were handing out pro-government leaflets, the government was half communist, while the Gaullists were old soldiers and those who had fought in the French Resistance.

[At this point Amina proposed inserting a series of six letters that she had written while in Paris and had published them in the Cheltenham Chronicle, the first appeared on Feb. 15th 1958. In the first five she appears to be acting mostly as a critic of art and drama events that were taking place in Paris. The sixth is different in that it relates to life in Greece and appears under her chapter relating to her holiday in Greece. An editorial decision has been taken to exclude the letters, as they do not relate to her life as such, coupled with the amount of space that they would take up and the fact that they have already been published. An unexpurgated version of the sixth letter appears in her chapter on Greece. Ed.]

In June I wrote home:

"The Colonel is out to dinner tonight so I am meeting Noelle and Othman at the Cité Universitaire this evening to go to a film. I was out there a few days ago, first we lay on the grass (This is a great luxury as it was about the only grass in Paris you are allowed to sit on) and listened to a nearby group of students playing records of Spanish music - the Sardana, a type of the round dance I saw near Barcelona. Then in Maison Tunisie we lay on Arabic divans eating red curry and tuna sandwiches and listening to Arab music."

Next morning I meet Noelle at 9 a.m. and we spend the day at Versailles. Othman will come here for a meal in the evening. By judicious buying in the market this morning, I got a good meal quite reasonably. Many of the fruit and vegetables we regard as luxurious in England are cheaper here when in season. I managed to get two pounds of asparagus for about 2/- a small chicken for 12/6 which we shall have with rice and mushroom cream sauce, lettuce 9d and a pound of small peaches for stewing about 2/-.

Saturday morning I am to get up about 5 a.m. in order to visit Les Halles (Paris's Covent Garden) with a Canadian girl who Noelle is at present sharing a room with at College Britannique (She left her 'family' last Saturday). Both Noelle and Othman will remain until the end of the month. It is arranged we spend the last evening all together but that they do not meet again before leaving, I am afraid it is going to be very difficult for them.

My mother visited me in June and I was able to show her many of the things I had enjoyed in the city. One evening we went to a fête de nuit at Versailles and saw the finest display of fireworks I had ever seen.

My Holiday to Greece

I had included an account of my holiday in Greece in the "Newsletter from Paris", but it was the unexpurgated version that went home to my parents in letters. They included some descriptions of the delightful things I saw, but also quite a lot about discomforts. I can only think that these were the early days of popular tourist travel and that it changed much in the years that followed. I wrote first from Kolokotrones:

"I have been enjoying myself ever since I came on the boat. At present I am sitting on the deck in Corfu Harbour, a few yards away there are two peasant women sitting, they have just come on board. They wear no shoes, finely pleated skirts almost to their ankles and white aprons, one has a white shawl over her head and the other a white headdress over elaborate rolls of hair, they are sitting on sacks of stuff and having their lunch off a tremendous loaf of bread and some bunches of grapes. It was a great relief to get on the boat, going through Italy on the train was ghastly. We changed trains at Milan and it needed six policemen to get us into our reserved carriage and even then it was a fight, tourists against the slum toughs of Milan. There was no restaurant car and only about one little trolley on the stations, which always seemed to be at the other end of the platform, we could get nothing. Some people traded packets of cigarettes for bottles of drinking water that men brought from drinking fountains, I did not think it wise to drink the water in Italy though I did finally fall for a sip or two, it was so terribly hot."

We disembarked at Patras and drove in a bus to a camp at Kyllini, to spend the first few days under canvas.

"The tent is O.K. the beds are iron which means no bugs, but the first night my room mate said she saw, literal translation, 'a great beast like a big yellow spider with big paws all round!' Fortunately I was asleep and did not see this horror. (Looking back I think this must have been a scorpion.) It is a flaw to the tent and tonight I am going to do it all round with my 'bomb' spray for insects. [Amina was an arachnophobe and never allowed her doors and windows to remain open. Ed.] The tents are amongst pine trees and scrub oaks on sandy earth. The restaurant seating about 100, is on a little cliff overlooking the sea where one gets a little breeze, the food is quite good. I swam this morning, then after lunch, very full of Greek wine, we both slept on the beach under the 'shades'. There are several shelters of bamboo mats on legs, because one is warned not to stay more than fifteen minutes in the sun, it is

unbelievably strong. One can see the island of Zante on the horizon. The shores we passed in the boat looked very savage wild country without a soul or a house or tree of any kind."

I often say the food is quite good, though as I remember it, it was mainly rice and tomatoes, sometimes the rice was inside the tomatoes and sometimes separately! However if memory serves me correctly the whole holiday, about eighteen days long, only cost about £28, so it is hardly surprising.

While we were at the camp site we were told that one evening there would be a fiesta or something at nearby Castro, so we went and it was an experience, though not one I would want to repeat. When we got there in a bus from the camp it was only three cafés, full of people and a little stall selling melons and sweets. There was a trio playing in one café, an accordion, flute and something else, so in the hope of seeing some Greek dancing Suzanne (my roommate) and I went up to it. Before we knew where we were we were sitting at a table in the crowd with five Greek men feeding us with nuts and their revolting ouzo drink. It was a very traditional vine hung verandah and Greek dancing by the men, similar to Yugoslavian but often very oriental with a dash of Russian in it. There was ordinary dancing too and the Greeks danced with us in quite a correct manner. They kept asking us to go for walks with them and one beside me with his arm across my shoulders kept pinching me! As they were getting more insistent we joined up with another large group from the camp for protection. They were suffering in the same manner and we all started looking for a taxi with the men from the camp trying to hold off the Greeks! I could not get rid of my persistent one and when he tried to pinion my arms to my sides and push me towards a dark street, I screamed and cried out 'Let me go' (in French which showed presence of mind) and hit him across the face with my handbag. A few minutes later he was back and I had Suzanne hanging on to one arm and him trying to drag me away with the other, by this time our men had found a taxi and packed all the girls into it to go back to the camp and get out of harm's way. We left with my persistent Greek waving happily through the open taxi window, they just don't take 'no' for an answer!

Next day we left at 8 a.m. on a bus to drive to Olympia. I think it was the following morning we had white 'butter' made from sheep's milk.

I wrote from Tripolis. . .

"Outside there is a brass band rather like a smartened up version of the Salvation Army, and every time black bearded priests go into a house opposite they play what sounds like a short jolly extract from Gilbert and Sullivan."

Not far from Sparta we visited Mistra, a ruined Byzantine village of the middle ages with several churches, some still containing frescoes. Situated on a rocky hillside overlooking the Plain of Lacedaemonia, the monastery of Pantanassa, with swag-like decorations on its walls, was memorably picturesque.

"I arrived back in Paris last night about midnight, after two whole days and nights on the boat and train preceded by two days journeys on mountain roads in the most terrific heat that I have ever experienced in my life. The air that came through the windows of the bus was literally like the hot blast from a furnace. It was extremely hot and airless in Athens but the last two days, from Athens to Delphi, and from Daphnis to Patras were the worst, I have never known such heat. The only thing that kept us all going was that travelling through the mountains all the time we struck about two clear springs of water each day. We used to drink it out of our hands, bottles, anything, stand in it, wash in it, almost worship it, one could certainly understand the significance of it for the ancients if the climate was the same then. Every time I got out of the bus my dress was wringing wet with sweat, the men started travelling without shirts while in the bus and everyone began to get exhausted. This coming immediately before the journey back meant we were just about all-in when we reached Paris."

After all this you will begin to wonder why I take holidays abroad, but really it was worth all the inconveniences. It is difficult to say what impressed me most. We certainly travelled through some very wild and isolated country. One saw all over the Peloponnese grapes drying laid out on the ground for currants, and in the Plain of Argos plantations of tobacco and the leaf strung out in rows to dry, also cotton growing which I had not seen before. At Delphi I picked ripe figs and saw pomegranates growing, somehow I never imagined they grew on trees, though I don't know what I did expect.

I suppose it was inevitable having travelled so much with Ron that I should often think of him in discovering a new country; when we passed peasants weaving by the roadside and women spinning as they walked beside their donkeys I knew how interested he would have been. I sent him a card from Athens.

After going to the open-air theatre one evening . . .

"We went to the museum in Athens which has a wonderful collection of Mycenaean jewellery, gold cups, tomb masks etc. The second day we drove to Mount Sounion. a temple high on a cliff overlooking the sea and the Islands of the Cyclades, We first joined a company of Greek soldiers who were dancing their national dances and singing in a café beneath an awning. They dance, men only, in a long line or circle, the leading man holding a handkerchief and performing all sorts of complicated steps with claps and finger snapping. Then some danced two together or alone. It was all very pleasant and friendly with the officer joining in from time to time. Afterwards we bathed in the sea, and Suzanne and I got stuck on a cliff, could not go on and were rather afraid to go back. Three of the soldiers were down below on the rocks and one of them came up and helped and guided us down in a most gentlemanly fashion. Once on firm ground with much smiling and thanking we shook hands all round, though of course we could not understand a word the other was saying. In Delphi we spent the night in a Greek house. It was very clean they had obviously done their best with poor material. I washed under a tap in the yard, which was probably preferable anyway to the wash basin which was in unpleasantly close proximity to the other amenities, which were questionable. The whole trip was quite well organised and we had iron beds all the way, so I still have not seen a bug. But we were very glad of my mosquito net which we put over the window each night and my insect 'bomb' with which we soundly dowsed the tent each night. I bought a magnificent pair of earrings a copy of those worn by the first queen of Greece. I should have liked to buy a woven rug but did not see one I liked until the last day and then I had not enough money left to buy it. I think I spent most of my 'spending' money on lemonade, and meths for brewing up tea or coffee each night. I must have drunk gallons of Greek water, though the Colonel and Mrs F said one must not drink it, however I did not suffer unduly. When there is no alternative but wine and fizzy lemonade to slake ones thirst, what can be done? I took plenty of formalin tablets to counteract its effects."

Getting back to Paris was as difficult as getting to Greece and one can only imagine that popular tourism was in its infancy then and must have greatly improved in recent years. After arriving back I wrote home on August 26th. . .

"I intended to tell you in my last letter how quickly one picks up the frantic habits of the French and Italians. I was with Colette in Brindisi on the return journey from the holiday and we had gone to a restaurant to pick up our packed meals which we had already paid for in Kyllini. We just had a stand up fight practically to get our seats on the train and were in no mood to be trifled with. I gave tickets for Suzanne and myself and then received two packed meals and a bottle of Chianti, Colette was given only a packed meal as they said there was only a bottle of wine between every two people. She started to argue, saying didn't people who travelled alone get anything to drink and before I knew where I was, in a restaurant full of people, I found myself arguing far more volubly than I ever thought possible for me in French, and waving my arms in the air like a fishwife! We got results, in fact it is the only way to get results there; finally he pushed a bottle into Colette's hand and said, using the rudest possible vernacular 'Get out, get out, take the bottle and get out!' And really we're both such nicely brought up, quiet girls!"

Noelle in Arab costume

In 1959 I Stay with Arab Friends in Tunisia and Go to Rome to See Etruscan Tomb Paintings and Early Christian Mosaics.

I left my job in Paris in October. I should have liked to stay longer, but my father had not been well for some time, and in the event he died of cancer, some eighteen months after I returned; I was therefore glad I came back when I did.

Noelle and Othman never met again and when, years later, Noelle was in Tunisia and called at his office it was only to find that he had died a few months before.

I had been pressed by both Othman to visit both him and his family in Souse, and also by Noelle to go and see her in Rome. In June I wrote home:

"It was a quite incredible thing that I was having a traditional English Sunday dinner with you one day in our own home, and twenty-four hours later I was deep in an Arab souk (cross between a market and a shopping centre) in quite another world.

We were a little late arriving in Tunis and some time going through customs. Othman and his wife Zakia were in the lounge to meet me and we set off in Othman's car which is cream and we all sit comfortably in the front seat, it seems to be just about the nicest car in Tunisia. They took me for a walk round the old Arab town and through the Souk. I am so lucky because I should hesitate to enter them even with a European man. The quarter was out of bounds to British troops during the war and is like a rabbit warren with little narrow streets, sometimes covered, sometimes open; but although people look at me no one has even begged while I am with Othman and Zakia. I cannot tell you what the colours are like in the Souk. There was one covered street, arches on each side supported by red and green columns and arched over the roof with a snowy white ceiling and on each side rugs, blankets, carpets and shawls of every brilliant colour imaginable, each shop or stall in charge of men wearing robes and red hats or turbans. In Tunis the women all wear the white robes (made by hand, like everything else) and hold one corner across the face or over the mouth or wear a black mask below the eyes, or sometimes draw a black material completely over the face leaving only a narrow slit for the eyes. It is quite extraordinary to see a white robed phantom with a blank black face coming towards you!

Some women wear high heeled shoes with the robes but mostly flat sandals or mules. The souk are very large each with their own quarters for one particular trade. In one street you see little 'caves' on each side under the arches, shoes being made or shirts, or brightly coloured camel saddles. Another part is all people making saucepans or weaving rugs or making jewellery or little 'fez' hats which are made white and then dyed red. At one point we turned up a narrow white street to the tomb of the man who founded Tunis, forbidden to non Muslims, We spent the rest of the day in the Arab quarter apart from a sortie into the European sector, walking, talking or sitting at café tables to rest. All the carts are pulled by very fine horses, very thin, but beautiful horses. One particularly passed us with red and gold decorated harness and the lower legs painted orange with henna, a very fine turnout. The air smells of the spices and peppers used in the cooking. There are a good few sheep about because unfortunately it is the sheep celebration (the feast of the sheep) while I am here. At the moment flocks are being brought in from the country and each family during the next few days will buy one sheep. They lead it off on a string, often tying a bow on the top of its head, and it goes off to live as a pet in the family until the day. You can see them eating boxes of hay outside doors of the houses carefully watched over by the children. I must say I have not seen one case of cruelty here, no more than one would see in any English market, in fact on the whole they seem more careful, and I saw one man rush in front of a lorry himself so that it would not run over his sheep, on the assumption I suppose that whereas it might run down the sheep it would hesitate to run down a man.

We stayed in Tunis for the night in the home of Othman's parents who are in their summer house at Monastir on the coast. Next morning Othman took us to the Bardo Museum and Zakia took me round while he went off to work. We are getting on better than I could have hoped. She told me lots about the Arab things in the museum and the Roman mosaics are just magnificent. They seem to take breakfast one step further than the French as we just went to a café and had each a glass of white coffee. We arrived at the museum about 8 o'clock and sat under palm trees and in an orange avenue until nine when it opened. We lunched about 12.30 on very hot (pepper) Tunisian hors d'oeuvres and prawns as long as one's hand. After resting a considerable time over coffee we drove to Sousse. The first day after walking a long way they said would I like a cup of tea, I was dying for a good drink, but one never gets it, because when it came it was a tiny little glass of stuff, like a mixture of strong tea and peppermint!

It is about 40 miles to Sousse and I saw my first camels including baby ones grazing in the fields. The prickly pear are in blossom and there are lemons on the trees, the crops mostly vines and olive trees. Although the women wear white the country women are very colourful, wearing red or striped robes and enormous pieces of gold and silver jewellery. The maid here wears dark maroon robes tied up girded round her, bare feet, hand woven pink and white jacket under the robes and a bright turquoise head scarf with lots of black hair falling villainously round her face and barbaric silver jewellery, we say 'bonjour' to each other which is all the French she understands. The children are all charming and so good, for the most part you would not know there was a child in the house let alone six. Naziah speaks French with me quite happily and the youngest follows me about mutely rather like Kitto does, waiting outside the bathroom door until I come out. I spent the morning in the kitchen with Zakia learning how to make couscous and Tunisian salad, so you'll be for it when I come home. I am to watch several times then to make the couscous myself to see if I can do it! Nowadays one can buy couscous ready made in supermarkets in England but we used the powered semolina and with a flat damp hand rubbed it into a sandy texture on a flat surface. This had to be twice steamed to cook it. Later this afternoon she is going to take me shopping with her. Nothing has a fixed price here. It was funny on the journey, we stopped at some wayside stalls (obviously to buy something) then both sides assume a 'couldn't care less' attitude as though buying some fruit had never entered their heads - everything is then tasted and pronounced to be no good and then after a great deal of haggling with several stall keepers some fruit was bought. White mulberries and some rather poor and tasteless things that look like yellow scrubby apples and are full of stones. I think this is about all for now. I believe tomorrow we are to go south to Kairouan and Sfax, and there is some mention of going to a fair tonight"

"I know you will be waiting to hear from me again, but so far we have had so many expeditions that there has been very little time for writing. I am having an absolutely wonderful time, and a thousand times more interesting than I could possibly have as an ordinary tourist. We went to a soireé given at the Sousse fair by the Americans last night and an Englishwoman told me she had driven round the Arab part of Tunis, I thought well she could not possibly have driven round the parts I've been to, we penetrate for hours into warrens of zouks. It would interest Granddad because all the shoes, mostly mules and sandals, are made by hand by shoemakers, often sitting in tiny little holes, where they could

not stand up straight, but in the streets given over to shoes, the smell is very familiar just like Granddad's workshops. I am particularly pleased that Zakia and I seem to be getting on really well as the situation was a bit tricky, this makes me very happy. I help her with the cooking and am now able to make the soup and salad unaided as it is very much the same every day. At present I have left her squatting on the kitchen floor cooking fish over a kind of flower pot full of charcoal, Having stayed in Madrid is a great help in getting acclimatised here. The fish is singeing well in clouds of smoke no wonder the dishes often taste peculiar!

We have just had a wonderful two day trip. On Friday we motored to Sfax by way of El Djem to see the Amphitheatre; it is very moving to see this great building which once seated 60,000 people in a region which now supports only a village, dwarfed at the foot of this colossus, in an area which is almost desert. Afterwards we went to the site of a Roman villa nearby where I picked up a few pieces of painted plaster from the walls and Othman afterwards presented me with a nice little pot in two pieces, which he had taken for me as he knew I would not take it myself. I have never before found a country where Roman remains and mosaics simply lie around on the ground in heaps! Zakia and I went round Sfaz in the afternoon while Othman worked. Most of his work seems to consist of sitting outside a café for hours, until a couple of car loads of young men from Service Topographique appear and he tells them what to do next, then sometimes we meet them on a journey where they are measuring the road with their three-legged things all set up, the head ones wearing topees (a lightweight helmet or sun hat). Everyone is very kind, Zakia and I were taken up the tower of the hotel de ville, and if on our travels we meet any particularly colourful characters with camels Othman and Zakia talk to them and they always pose happily for photos, nobody has ever held out their hand to me and even when I have offered sweets to little boys they have shaken their heads and gone all shy and have had to be persuaded. Zakia and Othman stayed the night at Service Topographique and they put me in a nearby hotel, then catastrophe! I'd left my passport at Sousse (not knowing we should need it). Finally the hotel people said they would phone the police and providing I had my carte d'identité Anglais perhaps I should be able to stay. In an inspired moment I proffered my British Museum reading room ticket and they solemnly wrote out the number of it as the number of my passport!

Next day I rose at 4.30 a.m. as Othman was calling for me at 5 a.m. We set off 100 miles into the interior towards Algeria to visit Sbeitla, the remains of a whole Roman town with an Arc de Triomphe, three temples, baths, houses, wide paved roads and a theatre. We spent a very happy morning there and had a picnic for lunch. We then motored back about 100 miles to Sousse, then a hurried meal and then a kind of cocktail party in the evening, by which time we were about dead with fatigue.

Today I did not get up until around 11 a.m. and should be quite content to repose a little but we are to visit Monastir "for the fête" which is probably something to do with the feast of the sheep on Tuesday. I believe we are to spend part of this week drying meat in the sun, both the country and the household are a fantastic mixture of old and new"

This week we are staying in Sousse as it is the feast of the sheep and there is much work for Zakia, but I gather we shall not be here after Sunday, as Othman is working in Tunis, so we are all going there early on Monday looking at some Roman remains on the way. He works there up to and including Thursday and I leave 9 a.m. Friday morning in order to reach Rome for the weekend as Noelle has a long week-end free.

Can't remember what I told you in my last letter but since then life has been getting more and more Arab, I am certainly being able to see the country from the inside rather than as an onlooker. Sunday last we went to Monastir to visit Zakia's mother and Othman's family, Zakia's mother lives in the Medina (Arab town). To get there one goes down a narrow alley and through a heavily carved wooden door (at least Zakia and I do; men can only enter the house if they know all the women very well), and through a small room into the square central court with doors opening on all sides, a well in one corner. There are heavy iron ornamental grilles over all the windows with stone carving above the doors and coloured tiles on the floor and so far up the walls. One goes straight across the courtyard into the room opposite and sits on a wooden sofa in an alcove facing the door. The younger female relatives, all with lots of children, wear European dress but all the older women wear the traditional costume. Every so often a heavily veiled woman comes in from outside, salutes you by a kind of airy kiss on each side of the face and allows the kind of heavy cream coloured counterpane they are draped in to fall to the ground, as they settle for a good talk. The effect of this I at first found quite electrifying, though I am now used to it. Almost all of the older women dye their hair with henna so that where it goes grey it is brilliant orange and this above all their gold jewellery is at first quite a shock. Both Othman's mother and Zakia's cousin each wear a large gold necklace elaborately mounting five English sovereigns. Everywhere you call you are served with sweet coloured sherbet and little sweet cakes. The house at Monastir, owned by Othman's family, is beautifully situated, overlooking the sea not far from president Bourgiba's house. His father is a charming man who speaks fluent French and has travelled a good deal. That evening we brought the sheep back, I did not look at it more than I could help, knowing that sooner or later it was going to turn up for dinner. Tuesday was the day and I had got myself all ready to accept the fact that he had to be killed. It is no worse for the animals than dying in the normal course of events I suppose. He was tethered on our terrace in the shade with food and water. But imagine my horror when next morning I found a calf there as well! The day of the feast I found very disappointing. I declined to attend the killing, later watched Zakia squatting over a little charcoal stove grilling lumps of meat for the children, they squeeze lemon over it and eat it with their fingers. Most of the morning passed like this with needy people coming to wish them a happy celebration and going off with packets of meat as presents. There was then great preparing of the 'feast' that I thought was going to be something good. I cooked lunch for Othman and I as Zakia was too busy to have any. From about 5.30 to 8.00 we made a somewhat dreary round of ceremonial calls imbibing unending quantities of this ghastly sherbet, all in our very best clothes. About 9.00. I thought the feast was ready at last - but was sadly disappointed to be served with a third rate faggot made from entrails with semolina couscous. It is the traditional dish but took an awful lot of preparation and tasted like nothing it was practically cold! We all changed back into our old clothes and prepared to spend the night cutting up and preserving meat. Othman chopped the bones, Zakia cut up meat and the maid and I put a large part of it through rather inefficient mincing machines. If you had ever tried putting the best part of a large calf through a small hand mincing machine you would realise it is not so easy as it sounds. The meat left on the bones is salted, then dried for a week in the sun and then stored in oil. I expect Granddad would enjoy it! I asked why they go to all this trouble and they say it gives the meat a different flavour - I bet it does! We were on until 1 a.m. Today there is great making of sausages which are also hung in the sun - that may explain why we did not like the Spanish ones.

Don't think I have much more news for the moment. Hope everything is all right at home."

I Visit Noelle in Rome.

The next letter was posted from Rome. Noelle had invited me to visit. She had a job teaching there and was living in a very nice apartment with an Italian girl who was married to an Englishman. I slept on a mattress on the floor, which was comfortable enough but not so good that, although the flat was scrupulously clean, at night a large number of cockroaches came out all over the floor. I was anxious to see, if possible, more Etruscan tomb paintings, and wanted to visit early Christian mosaics.

"I have been having a nice restful week-end with Noelle..... she was free until Tuesday and we thought of going to Tarquinia but Noelle is trying to organise an Italio-American friend, known as Willy, to take us sometime in the car as this would be much easier. Saturday we woke fairly late and talked so much over breakfast that when we looked at the time it was 12 o'clock! The shops are open from 4.00 to 8.00 so in the late afternoon we went round some exciting shops. This street is a turning off a larger street with small exclusive boutiques selling most marvellous clothes and accessories. I was very impressed with one of the larger cheaper stores and wish I could do all my Xmas shopping here, the trouble is getting it home. I have already burdened myself with a pot from Tunisia about 20 inches high in coarse white earthenware. It only cost about 3/- and would make a wonderful lamp base or decoration just as it is. However I must try to bring some glass back with me, the cheapest type of green Murano glass here is very contemporary in style, the glasses are with heavy bases. One can buy a beautiful carafe and 6 glasses for about a £1, just like the Danish glass which costs about £4 or £5 in England, and a tall thin jug about 16 inches tall for 10/6. The design of the china and glass is really superb. Beautiful tea-pots here, how often do you see a really good tea-pot in English shops? This is an odd thing when we are the tea drinkers. Yesterday we went to Ostia Antica, the remains of an entire Roman town, some of the houses preserved to the second story. There were wine shops with marble counters and bowls on them, marble tables, fountains, stables, mills with the stones for grinding corn. All in brickwork, giving an impression of what must once have been a busy town, but without the majesty of Sbeitla. We walked about it for five hours until we were exhausted and my hay fever very bad owing to a lot of tall grass about. This morning we slept until about 12.30, finished lunch at 4.00, so we do not feel so tired now and today there is a cool breeze though yesterday was terribly hot and heavy. It is a very nice part of the town, quite near the Spanish

Steps and everywhere quite accessible from here, from a park nearby one can see right from St. Peter's to an enormous white building on the corner of the street that leads to the Colosseum. Yesterday we passed through the area I knew from my first trip here.

While in Tunisia I spent another morning photographing the Roman mosaics in the Bardo Museum. I tried to get a hand-made copper or brass tray in the Zouk as a souvenir but I could not find a plain one such as I would like, so in the end I bought a hand-made kind of flat dish in copper on which one makes a paper thin pâté of semolina and water by 'bouncing' the paste on and off the hot copper, then you wrap sweet or savoury fillings in it and fry in deep fat and it's very good. I also bought a lucky 'hand of Fatima' door knocker and a piece of wood carved in patterns for pressing on cakes or pastry, all good simple Tunisian things which I prefer to brass trays made in Birmingham or elaborate leatherwork."

"Seems impossible that tomorrow I have already been in Rome a week. We had wonderful good fortune yesterday a friend of Noelle's, a pupil of hers, gave us two tickets for the first performance of Lohengrin, the Wagner opera, in the open-air theatre at the baths of Caracalla. It was superb, it is the largest stage in the world and the auditorium seats 10,000. The seats were very good, we think they were in the section at about £1 each. It was quite the most magnificent production I have ever seen. The back scenery is 39 feet high and in the second scene was built like a castle and the great wings of the ruined baths made it seem to merge into three dimensions. The scene started with little light and later as if the dawn were coming, there was more light and lights like lanterns moved about among the castellated top of the wall, and lights appeared inside the 'castle'. Four trumpeters came out on a balcony above the central doorway and blew a fanfare, eight horses were ridden through the doorway followed by soldiers in long red cloaks, then blue and gold, then medieval noblemen until the stage was filled with people. There must have been about 200 or more on the stage I should think; then a procession of monks in white bearing lights, then in long red robes wound down the stairs from the castle and finally the bride and Lohengrin in magnificent white and silver costumes. Very often throughout, it was like an old master come to life the colours of the crowd-scenes were so wonderful. In one quiet scene with only two singers on the stage a white cat chose to go right across the stage from one side to the other, he carried off the entrance with great presence. The opera started at 9.20 and finished at 20 past 1 a.m. However, we

were able to get a bus back to the end of our street and although it was fairly cold, we kept ourselves warm with little bottles of hot coffee and brandy in the intervals which really warmed the cockles of your heart. Today I went to the Roman National Museum, which has some very fine Roman wall paintings.

Sunday. We had an enjoyable day yesterday we went with a married couple, friends of Noelle's, in their car to Santa Severa on the coast. It is a charming village with a castle right on the shore; we left Rome early, at 8 a.m. We had a bathe when we arrived though the water was very cold. Then we drove to Cerveteri to see the Etruscan city of the dead with the great round tombs. This is one of the places I particularly wanted to see and it was very beautiful with butterflies, dragon-flies, and lizards in amongst the ruins which are covered with flowers. I found it most interesting though really I should have liked to spend a whole day there, but we were anxious to make use of the car and it was very kind of them to take us. We went back to the beach and spent most of the afternoon swimming and sunning on the rocks. We had lunch at a trattoria in Cerveteri, indifferent food as in most Italian cafés, but some fine local wine, which is almost black and tastes very much like Beaujolais. There is a little trattoria here at the back of the apartment and from our kitchen one can see a corner of their yard with tables under the trees, it looks quite picturesque. This afternoon we walked over to an old part on the other side of the Tiber, to Trastevere and on the way back we passed Casa Pallotti and the district I knew before.

I have a great deal to fit into the next week as there is so much to see. Want to get up early tomorrow and see as many churches as possible for mosaics."

The Following Saturday.

"I have just received Daddy's letter, thank you very much. Glad to know everything is all right, even if everyone is very busy. Mission here is pretty well completed. I have spent a quiet week looking at and photographing mosaics in churches and going to a good deal of trouble to obtain permission to photograph in the tombs at Tarquinia. After several visits to the Villa Guilia Museum and various 'phone calls I was successful. Noelle's friend has been too busy to take us in the car so this morning we rose at 6 a.m. (after going to bed at 2 a.m. which I'll tell you about in a minute) and caught the 7.30 bus from some distance over the town. When we enquired at the museum at Tarquinia they told us to hire a taxi, but knowing other people must be going in their cars we hoped to get a lift. Fortune smiled on us and I found a very nice American lady (art teacher) who was going on the visit alone in her car except for a lot of luggage, so we squashed in and about six cars set off in convoy with the guide in the first one. There is nothing above these tombs and they are quite unlike Cerveteri. There is simply a little wooden hut-like place built over the stairs and one goes straight down. In general the tombs are about 8' x 10' and painted all round. They really are wonderful, though one is already familiar with the majority of well-preserved paintings through reproductions. They were, on the whole, smaller than I had imagined. I do hope the photographs come out all right There are four 'tombs' transferred to the museum in Tarquinia including the very beautiful one of women dancing and men playing musical instruments. I have wanted to see these paintings for years, so it really has been quite a day.

We also had great good luck yesterday as a pupil of Noelle's, who has a relative who works at the opera house, gave us two tickets for the first night of 'Aïda' at the open air theatre that we went to before. The seats were very good and the production even more spectacular than 'Lohengrin'. The story is Egyptian and in the triumph scene there was a whole army, eight horses ridden, and then a wonderful moment, a chariot drawn by four chestnut horses was drawn onto the stage from side-back at a gallop, the horses stamped and tossed their heads all the time they were on. When the general had alighted from the war chariot, it turned in an arc and the horses galloped off again. I thought this was no mean achievement to get four horses from standstill to gallop in so small a space. In a late scene there was moonlight on a moving 'river' Nile and a real camel, they really beat the Americans at their own game when it comes to spectacle. There were also about 30 slave dancers, rather like mummy in the 20s. The singing was stronger and more moving than in the previous production so it was a very enjoyable evening.

I am leaving here on Wednesday morning and as I have been able to buy the slides I wanted here, I shall not go to Florence. Have managed to book a couchette from Rome to Paris, only costing just over a £1, and no change so the journey should be fine."

One of my reasons for going to Rome was to look at early Christian mosaics because I have always found the change over from pagan religions to Christianity fascinating. Nowhere do you see it more clearly defined than in the Mausoleum of Constantia (Church of St Agnes), built by the Emperor Constantine for his daughter. It is in the N.E. of Rome off the Via Nomentana, I remember making a very long walk to see it. It was built between AD 337 and 350. Every year the Roman Emperor selected an official religion and it was Constantine, probably in 313, who chose to make Christianity the official one, giving it the same privileges as the state pagan religions.

The building is round and in the form of an earlier pagan mausoleum, as for instance the one made for Diocletian in what is now Split. Inside, the mosaics, that decorate the barrel vault that runs round the interior between the outer wall and a series of double columns, depicts the Vintage with cartloads of grapes and workers treading the grapes, with an overall background of vines and cupids and a bust of Constantia in the centre. Other parts of the vault show figures, birds and cupids which, like the Vintage, were already familiar subjects in Roman mosaics before they were used for Christianity.

Alongside Santa Constanza are the ruins, only the walls remain, of an early basilica-type church. These were rectangular and derived from a Roman meeting place or basilica (basilikos Greek for kingly). This became the typical form of the Christian Church.

The other church that I found of particular interest was San Clemente, it is near the Colosseum on the Via San Giovanni in Laterano and is a very typical early Christian basilica, with one aisle on each side of the nave. The altar in front of the apse, which in pagan times had been used for sacrifices of animals, or libations, became adapted for the celebration of Christian rites. The church was built over a 4th century church, and below that are the remains of a temple to Mithras.

Looking at Palaeolithic Cave Paintings in the Pyrenees.

On August 14th to 28th in 1964, I joined a Workers Educational Association, Western District study holiday looking at Prehistoric cave paintings in the Pyrenees. It had a serious intent and the party was accompanied by an archaeologist and a museum curator, E. J. Mason and W. N. Terry. In the mornings we listened to lectures on the paintings and in the afternoons, and sometimes for the whole day we went on expeditions to the caves. We received lectures and were often guided by Mons. Romain Robert, a well known expert on Palaeolithic art, who discovered it in 1956, and together with Mons. M Nougier, the Cave of Rouffignac.

We should remember the caves and the paintings for the rest of our lives, but as a letter that I sent home to my parents showed, we also had a wonderfully jolly time. I have never made so many friends on any other holiday in my life, perhaps it was because we all came from the West Country so lived fairly close to each other. Certain it was that several of us became friends for life and I can think of three of their funerals that I attended.

[There is a surviving sheet of paper listing Mr Mason the tutor and the names and addresses of 18 members, who took part in the trip. The sheet is dated August 1964, Amina Chatwin, Bernard Rawes, Cedric Neilsen, Derek Jackson and Miss V Lyster-Smith are those from Cheltenham. Ed.]

We travelled in an old Dakota; I was often travel sick in my youth but this was the only time that I remember being upset in an aeroplane. I can only imagine that tourist travel in those days was a good deal more spartan than we expect today.

I wrote home to my parents from the Chateau de la Vergnière, Foix, in the Ariège:

" *It is very difficult to get down to write to you as I am never really sober after lunch. We are having a very nice time shedding all our inhibitions and never short of congenial company. When we arrived the weather was bad and everyone was suitably shattered - we found a dilapidated chateau, very poor quarters with bats flying into the bedrooms, cold misty mountains, with pouring rain during the night, the whole situated at least four miles from the nearest village. L'Herm itself is only a few houses and a small village pub. I think we were all rather horrified, but now we are settled in it all looks much better. The food is good and the wine limitless.*

The journey went well - the four of us arrived in Bristol and met Mr Page (hereafter Ivan) at the hotel. We all went out to lunch in an Indian restaurant where we had a very good curry, but Derek Jackson passed out after it, during coffee, which rather shook us all, but he seems to have been all right since. Next morning the journey went well. We were three and a half hours in the air, flying over Weymouth, the Channel Islands and across France. First we flew at 6000ft at 185 miles per hour, ground speed, but then climbed to 9500ft over the Central Massif, to go above a storm. We started pitching and tossing all over the place and for the last half hour of the journey I was very sick. The stewardess held wet cloths on my head and at least I managed to be decently sick in the envelope provided, though my hands had clenched up so that I could not move them. We had been provided with a very nice cold chicken lunch, which in the end proved to be rather wasted.

Everyone was very depressed when we arrived, and Derek and I walked into the hamlet of l'Herm before supper. It is magnificent country and now that the sun has come out it is really wonderful.

On Monday we had lectures in the morning, and in the afternoon went to Foix and looked round the museum, not too successfully as it was a public holiday and there were too many people. At six we went to the Town Hall for a champagne reception by the Mayor. They have a great heart and the mayor's family and councillors of the town sang Ariège songs for us and we answered with English ones, then were requested to sing Tipperary and so it went on.

That day's total seemed to be two squat glasses of red wine for lunch, two glasses of champagne at the reception and three red wines in the evening - this is sufficient to keep up a rosy glow from lunch time onwards. Next day we had lectures in the morning and went down Labastide Cave where one travels two and a half kilometres in three different boats (changing boats twice) on a subterranean river, which passes various stalactites and stalagmitic formations, and is very interesting. After dinner I walked up to the local pub with Ivan and imbibed a little more, as there is really nothing else to do in the evenings, and we all come back singing.

Two of the men carried a piano into one of the larger rooms and I remember joining Bernard Rawes in a pseudo Spanish dance on the first evening, which he kept up for ages as a solo, and he seemed such a quiet man! I only had two hours sleep last night and we had to get up at a very early hour as breakfast was at 7.15 so that we could start off for Gargas cavern at 8 a.m. It is so difficult to get to sleep here as there always seems to be so much creaking of beds and noises of all sorts throughout the night. I am contemplating joining in a walk up a mountain in Andorra on Saturday, 8,000 ft high. I have taken to smoking gauloises too, [I had never known Amina to smoke. Ed.], so with such contrasts of debauchery and the outdoor active life, you can see that this is a change from home. We had a very nice four mile walk from Labouiche into Foix, past herds of cream cows with cow bells, little mountain churches and mountain scenery. Gargas Cavern was quite an easy one, containing almost undecipherable engravings and stencils and negatives of mutilated hands.

In the afternoon we went to St. Bertrand de Comminges where there is a fine Romanesque cloister. We were provided with a very good picnic lunch and a bottle of beer each. We also spent a day at Ampurias to see the Roman remains.

Well, I hope you find this coherent though hardly a letter of style; it will at least give you some idea of what is happening. There is very little time."

To which I had added a few days later:-

"Really hope all is well at home. Much love."

"Yesterday we went down Le Portel, a very difficult cave, especially when trying to protect a camera. For three hours we were going over boulders and stalagmitic formations, through narrow crevasses, up straight for five or six feet, then dropping down into deep holes covered in mud as everything is covered with a thin slippery coat of mud, very exciting but very stiff today."

In one of the caves there was a diverticule where we entered individually to join a French guide. It was noticeable how sharply the ladies exited this bit of the cavern. When it was my turn I discovered why. The guide's enthusiasm had become too much for him and he was intent on kissing each one of us as soon as we came in close proximity.

The walks home from the pub were entertaining. The hedges were often covered with glow-worms, why this was I did not know, I do not recall ever having seen any elsewhere. Then one night in particular there was a great display of shooting stars. I thought perhaps it was the location but I have since heard that shooting stars occur at a particular time, which I think was in August, though what causes this phenomenon I do not know.

We often danced in the chateau, the Gay Gordons, and set dances, I think I taught them the Lancers, then one evening there was a bit of a festivity in the little village and I spent most of the night dancing with a large half Danish man, who had joined us from Devonshire. He had a good sense of rhythm and I enjoyed dancing with him, it would be the first of many times. Before long he came to live in Painswick as a milk officer for the Ministry of Agriculture. I should lose my heart for the third time and he would be the focus of my love life for the next eighteen years.

Bernard Rawes at his archaeological site 1977

Industrial Archaeology
Brings Ironwork into my Life.

I must have been drawn to research at an early age. I began looking into "between the acts" entertainment in the London theatre of the 18th century. Perhaps it was not surprising; from my school days we had been taken to see Donald Wolfit and his Shakespearean company which came to the charming Frank Matcham theatre in Cheltenham, called in those days The Opera House. By the time I was training to be a ballet dancer I was taken from time to time to see various ballet companies including such performers as Alicia Markova and Robert Helpmann. It was also in those years that the Ballet Joss was introducing more modern types of ballet and they too sometimes came to Cheltenham. Exactly when I started to visit London and go to the British Museum Library I am not certain, but I have very fond memories of the great round building that was the Reading Room. My work first appeared in print in 1961 in the Ballet Annual through the good offices of J.S. Richardson, well known in the ballet world. He added his name to mine, writing an introduction in the first part of an article I had written on "John Weaver (1673 - 1760), the Father of English Ballet".

I had also been long interested in archaeology and I can see that both these things had a great influence on the years ahead.

After the W.E.A. trip to look at Palaeolithic cave paintings, I sometimes joined the Bristol and Gloucestershire Archaeological Society holidays, going one summer on a trip led by R.D. Abbott A.M.A. to Brittany. We saw the impressive alignments of stones at Carnac and various Megalithic passage graves, as well as going by boat to Gavrinis, an exceptional passage grave with most unusual carvings on the stones.

Some years later I should go to Ireland with Bernard Rawes to visit New Grange with its enigmatic carvings of spirals and I think we went to Dowth and Knowth. Bernard was a keen archaeologist, and dug and wrote up several sites around Cheltenham; I helped him and his wife Barbara near Belas Knapp above Winchcombe and again at Barnwood. I also went on a course near Cambridge largely for experience in archaeological digging. I met there a Poor Clare nun who dug in black robes and a white coif but donned forearm protectors when actually on site. I got on well with her and it must have been quite a sight to see her driving beside me in the open M.G.

Archaeology was born of antiquarians going back to medieval times. Historians had a heyday in the 18th century, but when did antiquarians become archaeologists? Perhaps John Aubrey could be styled the first field archaeologist riding out in 1663.

"The chase led us (at length) though the village of Avebury, into the closes there: where I was wonderfully surprised at the sight of those vast stones: of which I had never heard before: as also at the mighty bank and graff (ditch) about it: I observed in the enclosures some segments of rude circles, made with these stones; whence I concluded, they had been in the old time complete."

He later brought the stones to the attention of King Charles II and wrote a description of them for him.

Today we should hardly call the Victorian gentlemen who dug barrows, sometimes several in a day, archaeologists, more wreckers or seekers after treasure trove, but had it not been for them archaeology would not have been born. Archaeological societies began to be formed in the late 19th century. The Bristol and Gloucestershire Archaeological Society was founded in 1876, and since then archaeology has become the careful science that it is today.

Around the middle of the 20th century, archaeology would be linked to two other partners and Industrial Archaeology and Archaeometallurgy would be born. We were fortunate to be in at the beginning and began to realise that the remains of industry were worthy of study and record, and the term Industrial Archaeology was coined by Michael Rix. The Gloucestershire Society for Industrial Archaeology was formed in 1963-4 and I began to go to a weekly evening meeting at Stroud with David Bick and some other friends. On the way back, we would stop at the Woolpack for a convivial drink. Later I would become secretary and editor of the Journal and now, some fifty years later, I have the honour to be their President. I followed on David Verey, who wrote the two Pevsner books on architecture in Gloucestershire, the Cotswolds and the Vale and Forest of Dean and the Rev. Awdry who became famous for his many books on "Thomas the Tank Engine" and his friends, for children.

The lectures encouraged us all to do our own research, Cheltenham had no great industrial, past and at first I was at a loss to know where to turn my attention. Then I thought of the ironwork, which was literally on my doorstep and all over the town. I went to the library to get out a book on the subject but nothing existed. I began to look at it carefully. No dating of the early ironwork would have been possible had not Mr Cossens, the Post Master, made a map of the town in 1820 showing every house then standing. This map and one made by Merrett in 1834 proved invaluable in grouping and dating the earlier designs in the town. Ironwork can of course be easily removed or replaced so that it is not necessarily contemporary with the building it adorns. I dated no design on a single example unless it was obviously part of the architectural design and dated by deeds. Gradually a chronology emerged, an early period of wrought iron with designs mainly based on simple verticals, a middle period of elaborate wrought work and the introduction of cast balconies, and a late period almost wholly confined to heavy ornate cast iron.

No other town in the country seems to have such a wealth and variety of ironwork, Bath, which pre-dates Cheltenham, has almost exclusively Georgian ironwork of the 18th century. Brighton with early 19th century interior examples in the Regency Pavilion and later cast balconies on its buildings and much structural and ornamental cast iron on the sea front, cannot, along with other towns, boast the extraordinarily rich period of wrought balconies which Cheltenham produced in the 1820s and 1830s; while the ironwork of spas like Leamington or Tunbridge Wells seems contracted into insignificance when placed against Cheltenham's riches.

I spent many happy hours, map in hand, traipsing the streets of the town, photographing and making notes. Gradually, I found out where many of the designs had been made and began to think of publishing a small guide and history of the town's ironwork. By this time I had joined the Historical Metallurgy Society to further my knowledge of iron, and Roy Day who was editing their Newsletter, was able to lay out the text of the book for me. I took most of the photographs myself and gradually the book evolved as I brought the text, photographs, and drawings I had made together and designed the cover. I sought the various permissions that I needed to use photographs other than my own, and David Verey and R.F. Tylecote, who was then Chairman of the Historical Metallurgy Society, kindly wrote forewards for the book, it was printed by Adprint, Cheltenham in 1974. I had 2000 printed and a reprint of another 2000 in 1984, by which time the original retail price had risen from £1.50 to £4.50. I do not suppose I should have thought of publishing it myself had I not had a long standing friend, David Bick, who had published a number of books on mining that he had written himself.

The book was well received and I think the review that pleased me most was in *House and Garden* which said, amongst other things, that the book "has much of the charm of a sophisticated scrap book."

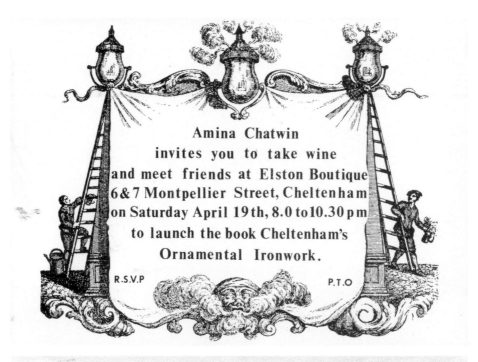

Amina Chatwin
invites you to take wine
and meet friends at Elston Boutique
6 & 7 Montpellier Street, Cheltenham
on Saturday April 19th, 8.0 to 10.30 p m
to launch the book Cheltenham's
Ornamental Ironwork.

R.S.V.P   P.T.O

Congratulations Amina !

At the Cheltenham Arts Council Awards ceremony held on 28th September at the Everyman Theatre Amina Chatwin was awarded a citation for her services to local history. Amina is recognised by all as the authority on Cheltenham's ironwork. Her book, *Cheltenham's Ornamental Ironwork*, written in 1974 and subsequently reprinted, must surely be the most referenced book in Cheltenham (or a close second to Gwen Hart's *History of Cheltenham*).

As a long-standing member of Cheltenham Local History Society Amina is always willing and available to provide help and guidance, giving freely of her time and allowing her collection of local ephemera to be used in displays etc. enabling others to share her experience and knowledge. She is a regular contributor to the Society's *News-letter* and has had several articles published in our *Journal*, including recollections of her childhood in Cheltenham and the town in wartime.

Her nomination for this award by Cheltenham Local History Society was supported by other local societies including Charlton Kings and Leckhampton Local History Societies and the Gloucestershire Society of Industrial Archaeology of which she has been the Society's President since 1993. Recognition for her work and especially her contribution to local history is long overdue.

Geoffrey North

108

Elston Boutique

At what point did my mother acquire a Morris Minor with a back that opened into a dickey seat? It may be that it first belonged to my father for there is certainly a photograph that shows him driving it. It must have been fairly unusual for a married woman to have her own car then, and it was all part of the dancing ethos. I know she used to drive to Stow-on-the-Wold and Cirencester to take dancing classes. It was still about by World War II.

From a business point of view, the war kept my mother busy. The town was full of service men and ballroom dancing was one of the main pursuits of their spare time. Looking back, I can see that she was something of an entrepreneur but at the time the family found her ideas something of a nuisance. At all events when 6 & 7 Montpellier Street came on the market, it had been a school of dancing, she decided to purchase it. She needed a mortgage and this turned out to be a problem. She had been running a successful business for many years but she was married and no one in those days would give her a mortgage unless her husband would stand guarantor for her, my father was a careful man and refused. It was not until the Cheltenham and Gloucester Building Society came to the rescue that it became possible - she obtained the mortgage and a new dimension developed. The school was no longer the Cheltenham School of Dancing but became Elston Studios.

A newspaper cutting preserved by my grandfather gave some idea of the scale of things that was developing, it even included a large party at the Rotunda building almost next door to the new studio.

Elston Studios New Year Festivities.

A very enjoyable evening was spent by pupils of the Elston Studios, at the Rotunda on Thursday, when a party of about 200 danced old time and modern to the Leslie Elston Trio.

The previous day 50 children spent a happy time at the studio party, entertained by the Roel Puppets.

At the Bingham Hall, a Christmas party was held for Cirencester pupils when Vyner Gomez and Phyllis Elston demonstrated South American dances in costume, which was much appreciated.

So this is the way things were going on, a number of assistants, a studio at Wellington Street, ballet dancing in the basement of Montpellier, and a large ballroom studio on the ground floor.

It was about eighteen months after that I returned from Paris that my dear father died of cancer. I had fought against being integrated into the dance school and was working at a shoe shop in Montpellier. I remember going straight from the shop to the hospital one afternoon to see him. He was very ill but I did not realise he was so near to death. I stayed with him for some time before returning home; it was only about half an hour after I arrived that they phoned to say that he had died. Had I only known what was to happen I should have remained as I should like to have been there with him when he went.

My mother used to do a lot of examining work in various parts of the country and one place that she went to had just opened a shop in their studio, it was a shop in the day time and a dance studio in the evening. Once she had the idea, nothing would do but that she should open a dress shop. At first, she sold only evening dresses, which was not economic. As far as I was concerned, the shop idea was a step too far and I could not stand by and see the chaos that was ensuing; I think I also felt that with my father gone it was time that I did something useful. I took over the management of the shop. We were expected to remove all the stock behind curtains at the end of the day for the evening classes. It was extremely inconvenient, to say nothing of getting it out again the next morning. It is not very clear in my mind now how the matter was resolved but before long there was a complete division, all the dancing took place in the basement and the dress shop became a proper one with a full range of ladies clothes.

Amina above her shop

Running the shop together was not a happy arrangement buying together was a disaster and only led to arguments and shouting matches. Gradually the dress shop became my responsibility and my mother confined herself to the dancing school and doing the books of the shop. I employed several part-time elderly ladies as assistants and one, who in her youth had been well trained in a large dress store, became a dear and invaluable assistant for many years.

Many people seem to think that running a dress shop must be a lot of fun - seeing all the new fashions, and since you are the owner taking a day off whenever you want to. I can assure you that nothing is further from the truth. It was hard work and usually started with sweeping down the front and back of the shop, once we became established it meant working hard all day, and not closing until 6 o'clock. Once I had made and eaten a meal, I might then need to spend the evening putting up hems or making various alterations to clothes so that the garments we sold would be a good fit on the customers. Fortunately, my grandmother had trained me well as a seamstress and I could have made anything in the shop.

I took naturally to display and enjoyed doing the windows, we had two large ones in the front and two small ones at the back.

Occasionally we gave dress shows but I found in the end that a far better way of advertising was for me to give lectures to Women's Institute meetings. These I did all over the county and in the end did more than 100. I used to show them how Irish tweed was hand woven, because in those days, amazing as it may seem, we sold excellent Irish tweed suits for only eight and a half guineas. I had also visited the factory where our knitted suits were made, and taken a series of slides; they were real classics and a completely different process to the tweeds. People remembered these talks and would come to the shop perhaps as much as six months later. We gradually built up a large and loyal clientele. I did not worry too much about the very latest fashions but looked more for wearable classic clothes that would last. Artificial fibres were beginning to come in but I favoured natural ones and much of our success was built up on Horrocks' cotton dresses, very well known and popular in their day. I used to spend about two days twice a year visiting London and buying at dress shows or show rooms and would also go over to Dublin. Their great idea was to ply one with Irish whiskey with the assumption that the more legless you were the more you would purchase and the larger your order would be.

AUTUMN ❧ ❧ ❧

Season of mists and mellow fruitfulness!

For us it's the glowing colours
and crusty textures of Tweeds

Rich berry reds and orange; hawthorn and rowan; or colours
subtle as stream-washed pebbles or lichen on old apple trees

Tweeds woven in the Outer Hebrides or in the whitewashed
cottages of Donegal, tailored into topcoats, suits and skirts

Dresses and scarves from The Crock of Gold
the softest and lightest wool in the world

Come and browse at

ELSTON *BOUTIQUE*

6 - 7 Montpellier Street, Cheltenham

Telephone 25086   Beside the Rotunda

ROGER WILSON

This did not really work with me as I had a strong head and my ballroom dancing days had made me used to spirits. I remember on one occasion being held up on the flight back and arriving late at Bristol Airport, so that I was late driving back to Cheltenham in the car and found the mini-bus full of models already drawn up outside the shop ready to go off to a dress show. These I compered so it was all go that evening.

Many hundreds of customers must have come through our doors in the thirty odd years we were open, yet only a few stay in my mind. There was the titled Cheltenham lady who must have grown rather absent minded, and one would find her petticoat strap held together by a diamond brooch but her dress held by a large safety pin, she had obviously used the first thing that came to hand.

Then there was an American lady who if she failed to like the colour of the garment she had tried on would say "Oh no, I look absolutely dug-up in that!" Another American, the wife of a well-known local industrialist, came into the shop with a friend when we were showing some new plaid capes from Scotland, and said it would be just the thing for walking the dog to which the friend replied "But you don't have a dog!"

There was a little old lady who wore ankle socks, rode a bicycle, and had been a suffragette; another had presumably been used to darkening her eyebrows but as she grew older could not see so well so that she always had two eyebrows one above the other, over each eye. Well, it comes to us all. I used to wonder why ladies could not stand on one leg when putting on clothes, but now I know. On the whole we liked our customers and got on well with them. I liked to see them well turned out in clothes that they would not get tired of wearing.

Then there were travellers who called to sell me merchandise and some became faithful friends over many years. There was one who started selling knitwear from Taiwan and when he showed it to a shopkeeper in Wales the lady said "Oh I know, just north of Talybont"! During the war he had fought, I believe, in the Western Desert and then all the way up Italy. In the north he met and fell in love with a young lady. After the war he went back and married her, and they returned to England, but when he retired they went back to northern Italy, Treviso I think, and his two sons worked in Brussels for the European Union.

I was a firm believer in advertising and the shop appeared on the screen of the local theatre, coining the motto "We Care what you Wear." We frequently advertised in the local "Echo", sometimes a little off beat. On one occasion we showed an old print of the Rotunda and allied the shop to the time when it was first built beside the Spa.

It must have been about 1971 when I put up an exhibition on the walls of the shop about "Fashion in Montpellier from 1800". On one occasion I brought my car into advertising use. After my father died I bought an MG Midget; it was much loved and I would drive it for the next forty years. In fact it was about the best investment I ever made; I paid £800 for it new with wire wheels and when I stopped driving its value was £7000. Every year there was a procession through the town and one year, with the hood down, I filled the car with naked window models, and drove from Pittville to Montpellier, it was quite eye catching. After taking over the running of the shop I joined the Chamber of Commerce and took a keen interest in its meetings; I also became the Hon. Secretary of the Montpellier Trading Association. We did a great deal to popularise the area; between the wars, it had become very run-down, and I really think our efforts were largely instrumental in bringing it back to life. For a while we ran a Montpellier fair each year with stalls all up the Montpellier Walk.

I have a copy of the lucky programme for the second year, 1977 when it took place on July 26th. There was live music and singing throughout the evening, and a number of linked events - a dog show, a children's fancy dress competition, a window letter contest and a "Miss Montpellier". Over in Montpellier Gardens there was an air-balloon and various events. The Fair was opened by Tom Shearer, an estate agent and Chairman of the Association, and Peggy Mount, an actress television celebrity. He said in his speech "The idea of the fair was to put Montpellier on the map and to bring you to this delightful 'village within a town' with its beautiful Regency architecture, its gardens, and above all, its wide selection of first-class shops with good parking facilities".

The whole thing was a fun occasion and was crowded with people and did much to popularise the area.

We had a wonderful milkman and when he started work it was delivery by pony-cart. I remember seeing these in my youth, on the way to school. Later it became a van and one severe winter when snow was piled high in the gutters, he could not get along his usual round and parked the van on the island at the top of Montpellier and people collected the milk from him there.

One day in 1985 when they were filming "The Whistle Blower" in Cheltenham, a story about GCHQ (Government Communications Headquarters), they had been filming a scene at the Wine Bar opposite the shop. I heard a slight commotion at the entrance and went to the front door to see what was going on only to find several people standing around and Nigel Havers sitting on the door step. "I hope you don't mind me sitting here" he said with his usual charm and I replied "You can sit there anytime", though a few weeks before I had turfed off in short order two refuse men who were sitting there eating their sandwiches! (Nigel Havers' very amusing autobiography "Playing with Fire" was published in 2006).

During the last few years at the shop I started what must have been one of the earliest mail-order services, selling cotton dresses, and shirt and skirt suits by Joanna Frances. I designed a fold-out leaflet, and it was very successful. I still have a few of the letters I received. One from a lady in Cornwall says "The arrival of a dress, I ordered only at the end of last week, by Monday morning's post, so astonished and pleased me that I found I must tell you so"!

And from Somerset "I feel I must write to tell you how pleased I am with the two dresses I have purchased from you recently. The quality and material used and the finish of the work is very good - no loose buttons for example"!

LONG OR SHORT SLEEVES IN THIS STYLE.

AMINA
Classic cotton suit made especially for us. Easy flare to slightly shaped skirt. Shirt collar faced to wear open if required. Can be worn tucked into skirt like a dress, or belted outside as a suit. Available in short or long sleeves. Short sleeves £47.50 Long sleeves £49.95.

Size 12 to 18   *Small all over typical* **Liberty** *floral.*

A. **Petrol** blue, peacock and maroon.
B. **Grape**. Mauves and blues.
Long sleeve suits made in A & B. Short sleeve suits made in A & B and also in C. **Geranium**, which is bright colours of red, turquoise, orange and purple.

Another from Plymouth,
"I just want you to know how pleased I was with my "Susanna" dress which I received just before going on a motoring holiday to Scotland. I wore it a great deal while travelling and despite this very hot spell of weather always felt comfortable and looked cool, crisp and uncreased."

While from London:
"Thank you for sending the dress I ordered so promptly. For years I have been searching London shops for classic cotton shirt-waisters, but little success, so last year when staying with my son in Derbyshire, I was delighted to find a "Joanna Frances" dress in the Ritz Gown shop in Belper. Then a few weeks ago I noticed your advertisement in the National Trust Magazine, and having ordered a dress and am once again delighted with it."

I believed in natural fibres and classic styles and it seemed that readers of that magazine thought the same way. The advertisement cost, I considered, a vast amount and was about the size of a large postage stamp but it was such a success that I never had to advertise again anywhere!

My mother had bought a small villa on the Atlantic coast of Spain. She did not live there permanently but liked to spend a few weeks at a time at the villa. I did not go much as there was nothing to do but drink with people or sit in the sun. The development, clustered round a large hotel, was mostly inhabited by English or German people. It was a few miles from the village and much of one's time was spent walking to or from it, either along the beach or on the cliffs. In the evening when the shadows were lengthening it was pleasant to look down on the boats of the fishermen coming in below. I had one holiday there with a half-Danish friend (from the Foix holiday). We bathed naked in the sea and walked miles along the coast, in the opposite direction to the village, through woods of Umbrella pines to a creek where Asphodel lilies grew.

My mother was 86 when she had gone there with a lady companion when she was taken ill with her heart. I was informed that she was in hospital in Cadiz and for several days tried to get her brought home to England without success so I went over and stayed five days with her in the hospital. It seemed quite different to our own hospitals with families tending to camp out around the bed of the person who was ill. It was difficult as my Spanish, although fit to buy a pound of tomatoes, was not really up to what was required. I remember struggling with a phrase book trying to say "Please let my mother depart in peace".

I had promised to bring her body home as in Spain they put you on a shelf in a cemetery for a few years and then presumably throw you on a rubbish heap. Everything was looked after by the insurance and her body in an impressive coffin came separately to an undertaker in Cheltenham.

Archeometallurgy

With ironwork firmly established in my life I felt the need to know more about it - how it was made and worked, so I joined the Historical Metallurgy Society and the British Artist Blacksmiths Association.

It was in 1969 that I joined H.M.S. and the first conference that I attended was in Penzance. The day before I had taken the train to London, in those days one could go return on the Cheltenham Flyer for 27/6 (£1.7.6.). On the return journey a gentleman got in at Reading. He was carrying a considerable number of small packages and I helped him to stow them in the net container rack above the table and seats, for we were in one of those long open carriages.

We had a most interesting conversation until he got off at Didcot. Next day I drove to Penzance and was surprised to find how long the journey took, it was further than I thought. I was rather late arriving and dinner had already begun. Next day when I walked into the lecture room who should be the first person I saw but the man I had met on the train! It was R.F. Tylecote senior lecturer in Metallurgy at King's College, Newcastle-upon-Tyne, who in 1962 had published "Metallurgy in Archaeology" the first book of its kind to be written in the British Isles on the Bronze Age to medieval times. He could not only be said to have invented the term "Archaeometallurgy" but also had a great deal to do with the setting up of the Historical Metallurgy Society, which soon became an international group of great importance.

We had a most interesting weekend, listening to lectures and being shown round old mining sites by J.H. Trouson Chairman of the Cornish Mining Development Association.

It was at this conference that I first met Roy and Joan Day from Keynsham. Before making our return journeys home we would spend some time on the beach taking an interest in the granite pebbles, and then go and look at the remains at the archaeological site of Chysauster, a settlement of 1st to 2nd century round houses.

The Historical Metallurgy Society had been formed in 1963 as a group of twenty seven members, because there was concern for the few remaining blast furnaces in the country which were rapidly becoming ruinous. The group which had been an offshoot of the Iron and Steel Institute, later became a society, with a journal which appeared twice a year. Its interest widened to encompass the study of pre-history and history of metallurgy appealing to historians and metallurgists all over the world, until it had 600 members in 34 countries. ("The H.M.S. in retrospect" by Richard Doncaster in History of Metallurgy Journal 23 number 2 1989.)

In the early years we visited many of the old blast furnaces, Duddon, Moira, Dolgun, Neath Abbey, and many more. Also ironworks at Blaenavon, Bersham, Blists Hill, Clydach and, of course Ironbridge was our stamping ground. I remember clearly the evocative Derwentcote cementation steel furnace before it was tidied up and partly restored.
We held conferences all over the country, listened to lectures and usually had a field day looking at mining sites of interest. We would go to the Forest of Dean for Darkhill and Whitecliffe furnaces.
There was Wealden Iron and Bristol Brass. I have happy memories of scrambling over stones with Michael Darby, a descendant of the famous Ironbridge family, and Richard Doncaster who took personal interest in the wild plants that grew on metalworking sites.

I remember standing by the river after we had held an A.G.M. in the Tower of London in 1984, where we had enjoyed looking at the armouries, when one of the members said to me "It is the only day in the year when I can talk to other people of similar interests.

Roy Day had been editing the H.M.S. newsletter for a number of years and I took it on in 1985 producing some fifty of them before handing it on in 2003.

Crossing Iceland 1966.

Many of my friends I have made from attending evening classes run by the Worker's Educational Association. On a geological course I met Ray Peel and we became friends for life. He was a chemical engineer with the Coal Board and liked old cars, but his great interest was in walking and mountain climbing. I joined him and a small group of his friends for a few days walking part of the Pennine Way. After two or three days I began to get rather tired of just walking and looking at the view and I borrowed one of the cars and went off alone to see the remains of the lead mining district of Middleton-in-Teesdale, and on another day I drove to Richmond, Yorkshire, to see the little 18th century theatre.

In 1966 he was going to Iceland with Tony Drake, who ran his family store in Winchcombe Street, Cheltenham, two other men from away and Betty. They needed someone to share her tent, which was how I came to be involved. It was not a particularly good time for me to go on such a trip as I had fallen down and broken my leg badly some eighteen months before.

We drove to Glasgow, and from there took a plane to Reykjavik. On the flight we had an excellent view of the island of Surtsey that had risen from the sea only two years before. In Reykjavik we hired a four-wheel drive Land-Rover, with much larger wheels than usual. We planned to cross the island basically driving for one day and then walking for a day; either camping or staying in one of the mountain huts where one simply walked in and took possession. It was a fantastic country, lava deserts of black sand, volcanoes and the most amazing waterfalls.

First we went to Thingvellir where from the year 900 they had in the past held their open air parliaments. It was some time during the beginning of the trip that we had our one good meal of the holiday in a hotel. It was salmon such as I have never tasted before or since. I should think they had fished it out of a stream at the bottom of the garden, it was just fantastic and we lived in hopes of finding such another meal but this did not materialise. For the most part we lived on the food we had taken, minted lamb in tins and suchlike. We made our way across the interior and we did not have another meal except of our own making until we reached Akureyri in the north. There we had lunch in a seaman's hostel, I cannot remember what I ate but I do recall that Ray had sausages, never a great meat eater, he was served about two lbs of them! There was prohibition in Iceland yet it was here that we kept seeing men absolutely dead drunk in the gutter.

Towards the beginning of the journey Ray, who was considered one of our most experienced drivers, saw a couple of pedestrians walking towards us, a very unusual occurrence. He was always polite and did so much bowing and scraping and trying to get out of their way, that he inadvertently drove the Land-Rover into the ditch! However, we soon had it out.

Often there was no road, just a track across the desert and one chose which track looked the best. It was in such a place that we met some Americans in a car, which was so unusual that we all stopped and the men of both parties talked. I suppose it was not surprising because we were driving an Icelandic vehicle and all our men had several days growth of beard, but I was none the less surprised to hear one of the ladies in the American car say to the other "What good English these Icelanders speak!".

Almost before we left Reykjavik we saw steam rising from fields and before long we were at Geysir, where a geyser shoots up about every ten minutes in a great height of spray. The waterfall of Gullfoss was my first surprise in Iceland. I knew there were large waterfalls but I expected that they would be long and thin. I was not prepared for a great expanse coming down in tiers and in the shape of Niagara Falls. Sometimes with a waterfall, the sun would catch the spray and a rainbow would rise up from the water.

At Hagavatn we spent some time climbing the stony slopes and from the top looked down at the most wonderful view of a river winding away, with mountains on the left, and on to the distant horizon.

It must have been as we approached a hut in which to spend the night, hear Kerlingarfjall that we met a young German called Jan. It was getting dark and the pack he was carrying was so large that when we first saw him in the distance I thought it was a great bale of hay. He asked if we could give him a lift to the hut and the men said there was no room and offered to take his pack, understandably he was unwilling to be parted from it and Betty and I pleaded that we should make room for him. In the end we set off again and he was sitting on top of his pack in the middle of the seats at the back.

He was a forester from the Black Forest and would spend the next couple of days with us. Next day was one of the most extraordinary days of the whole trip. Kerlingarfjall was a rift between snow covered mountains as we walked down to it, crossing a small river, it was all laid out in front of us with vents of steam rising along the rift. We walked up a very cold stream with always pools of boiling mud or water on each side. I had never set eyes on or even imagined such a place. Later it opened out and hill slopes rose from a floor of bright green moss.

Unlike the others I never walked or climbed mountains for the sheer joy of it. It must have been the day after because Jan was still with us when we climbed a particularly difficult cliff, the Englishmen left me to get on with it but the young German was pushing me from behind and saying "you can do it, you can do it" over and over again in an encouraging manner. When we arrived at the top I was not amused to find that we could have walked up to the top by quite an easy path from the back and saved ourselves all the effort!

We were going north to Akuraryri, we drove through quite a wide river where one had to drive into the water then down the middle of the river to a rock before turning at right angles up a slope to the bank. Long before you reach Akuraryri you can smell it. Long lines of fish hang drying on frames outside the town. As we approached the town it seemed laid out beside a wide river and I remember little of it except the lunch at the Seaman's Mission and the drunks that seemed to litter the streets. We spent a rather noisy night camped in the central car park. Next day we departed for Lake Myvatin. It is famous for the many sorts of ducks on the water though I do not remember seeing many.

What was impressive, were the jagged pillars of lava that rose from the lake at Dimmurborgir.

Askja was a great volcanic crater full of water, immense and silent, quite overwhelming.

The men were anxious to climb Mount Herdubreid, a flat-topped mountain 1,682m high. En route towards it we crossed a most dramatic landscape, a lava desert of very black sand overlaid with patches of white snow. Finally we came to the mountain hut we were aiming for, Betty and I would spend the next day there, resting and washing ourselves and our clothes. We were close to a small river and spent some time exploring it, there were many fine plants of Angelica. The men had a three-hour trek to reach the mountain and as they began to climb it they kept hearing avalanches of stones falling around them. I do not think they reached the top but it was very late before they returned.

We crossed one extremely rough lava field, and we could see why vehicles needed to be four-wheel drives.

We stopped at Glaumbaer to see typical old turf-roofed houses. Each of the inhabitants had a built in cot-like bed at the side where, by the window, they could see, for the ladies to do hand work and the men could carve during the winter days.

Dettifoss and Gullfoss were waterfalls no less impressive than Gulfoss had been.

We made our way down the western side of the island towards Reykjavik where I bought a lot of the distinctive Icelandic wool to make sweaters for Ray and myself. We went to the museum to see past treasures and I particularly remember the traditional costumes such as would have been worn in the houses with the turf roofs. In the park we would pose for a photograph of the group; it had been a memorable trip.

My First Visit to America 1982.

It was in 1982 that I first went to the United Sates, and wrote to friends about the very enjoyable time I had spent there.

"At the beginning of June I returned from a wonderful trip to America, travelling some 2000 miles while there, and going at least in part, through ten states, so I managed to see a great deal in eighteen days - knowing my interests you will not be surprised to know that it was ironwork all the way!

I travelled with a party of British blacksmiths, flying on the great curve over the Atlantic, northwards over Manchester and Belfast. We then flew over nothing but sea until the remote areas of Canada, somewhere by Goose Bay, ice in the sea and frozen rivers and lakes far below, before following the New England coast line down towards Washington; we were met at Dulles Airport by blacksmiths of the Guild of the Potomac. They looked after us wonderfully, offering us the hospitality of their homes, and showing us ironwork wherever the best was to be found; from modern Albert Paley work at Clyde's Restaurant near the big shopping mall at Tyson's Corner, to the historic Samuel Yellin ironwork in Washington Cathedral. I was put up two nights, together with Dorothy Bosomeworth (who had been arranging an ironwork exhibition at the V & A), by Ed. Jackson an astronomer from the Naval Observatory, and his wife Mary Ann, who spins and weaves. They have a house in a most delightful area, Garrets Park, where many houses are of wood in the 18th century style, dotted about a wood of very tall trees; when the dog pricked up his ears at night, they would say "there is probably a racoon outside". Throughout the trip the new and unknown varieties of birds and animals and trees were a great interest; I noticed on waking the first morning that all the bird songs were different. Incidentally, that had been quite a sleep, as time differences had meant that our first day had been twenty-three hours of activity.

While in Washington we were shown the Capitol, the Watergate Building, the Lincoln and Jefferson Memorials, and the White House. The iron gates of the White House have large hydraulic rams which rise up as soon as the gates are shut, so that any vehicle trying to ram them comes off worst. I was greatly privileged to see a wonderful cross section of American life; the second evening in Washington we were invited to an industrialist's mansion to take cocktails by the swimming pool. The next day the Jacksons drove us 400 miles, with forests all the way, to the

Artist Blacksmiths Association of North America conference in West Virginia, on the way we sampled McDonald's fast food, where all consumables come either in cardboard boxes or packets - it is true there is absolutely no incentive to linger over such a repast!

Throughout the five-day conference there were numerous demonstrations going on continuously, slide shows, lectures, films, it was impossible to participate in everything. The lodges were widely spaced around small lakes, where bull frogs croaked in the evenings with a background symphony of cicadas; a nice swimming pool, and nearby a campers area which included some Indian tepees. At the first meal I sat beside a young smith from Alaska, and a couple with two small children, from Colorado, who had travelled two and a half days by bus to reach the conference. Owing to some mix-up with the bookings, hardly surprising as I understand 600 people had booked, 750 had arrived! - we spent the first night at the Great Western Hotel in Ripley, nothing but garages, parking lots, supermarkets and innumerable motels why should anyone want to go there? Good breakfast in the morning, but no way could I ever face a staple American dish of sausages, pancakes and maple syrup at such a time - just as further south I drew the line at 'grits', what looked like porridge served with the bacon and eggs!

The best part of the conference is meeting with old friends from all over the world and making new ones of similar interests. It was a particular pleasure to contact people with whom I had only corresponded before, or with whom I had taken issue over minor historical niceties of iron making. It seemed no time at all before everyone was going on their separate ways again, and the smith from Nova Scotia, whom I had last seen in Hereford, was trudging off down the road with a pack upon his back, to hitch his way home.

Walt Billings, a sculptor and architectural metalworker, drove us the 450 miles to his home on Society Hill, Philadelphia where he showed us some of the considerable amount of ironwork to be seen on the buildings there. We met up with other members of the British group at the Yellin Museum, which is a wonderfully rich collection of ironwork. Next day we took a train back to Washington, and four of us lunched at Blackie's a quite fantastic restaurant, with real Tiffany lamps and authentic Art Nouveau stained glass, and need I say, ironwork everywhere. We ate succulent pinky red roast beef, sliced off an enormous joint, which oddly they always call Steamship beef.

Our host Bill Gichner, knew Blackie, who was too busy to see us, but we met his lady help, a southern belle in a close fitting pink suit, who just had to be, and really was, called Lu! We visited a small modern exhibition of Paley ironwork; then Gich drove Dick Quinnell (who has an ironworks in Leatherhead), and myself to a "Forge-in" at the headquarters of the Potomac Guild at Arlington, where they have built a guild forge at a nature reserve. Here the great Czechoslovakian smith Alfred Hammermann forged all the afternoon and evening, and sometime after 11.30 that night, we set off to drive to Delaware. We crossed the northern part of Chesapeake Bay (later I would cross the great causeway at the south) and they always said "We are going to the ocean", not the sea as we might say in this country - we arrived at 3.30 a.m. Next day on the deserted beach, stretching for miles, I knew why they had called it the ocean. How much grander, bigger, more impressive a word it is - this was the ocean; and it gave me as much of a thrill to see the Atlantic ocean from the other side, as it had done, years before, to ride overland from the dull grey English Channel to the brilliant Mediterranean.

I stayed two very happy days on the Delaware coast, all unexpected and wonderful hospitality, then took the bus from Salisbury to Charleston, a long overnight journey, but I slept better on the buses than I expected through North and South Carolina - change at Wilmington, then down the coast through Myrtle Beach to Charleston - which I adored. It is a most elegant town; a great deal of wrought ironwork, particularly characteristic 'pulpit' shaped balconies, straight each side and rounded in the centre. I took a 'buggy' ride round the town and walked and photographed a great deal, though the heat was intense. It was here that I saw a magnificent avenue of very tall magnolia trees.

At the end of the second day, I caught a bus to New Orleans, via Augusta, Atlanta and Mobile. It was a journey of about 23 hours and entered Atlanta at 2 a.m. It was a fantastic experience, I do not know what I had expected it to be like, rather as it was in "Gone with the Wind" I suppose, but I had been asleep and woke to find the bus in some sort of sunken routeway with great skyscrapers, the first I had seen, towering immediately above us, so that they seemed to lean at crazy angles, and with lights flashing everywhere; it was rather like entering some deserted city in space. It was quite a relief to find the people at the bus terminal normal - not little green men!

In the morning we approached New Orleans through a series of resorts like Biloxi Beach, then there seemed to be forests and swamps, I could see trees standing in green coloured water, and the great expanse of Lake Pontchartrain. I was not at first enamoured of New Orleans, it seemed noisy, dirty, and dilapidated after Charleston. I arrived in a tropical downpour and had to book in the first hotel, my black taxi driver suggested, in the old French quarter. It turned out to be not too bad a choice as experience showed it to be a far more expensive and touristy neighbourhood than anywhere else I had been.

It basically seemed to be poor negro housing interspersed with top quality and fiendishly expensive hotels and restaurants, a strange mixture. Anyway there was ironwork everywhere and after twenty-four hours I began to get the feel of the place and to find it more agreeable. I was delighted to find a firm still casting most of the traditional ironwork patterns. I took my breakfast at the Café du Monde, which is open 24 hours a day and sells only beignets, coffee and cold milk; there is undoubtedly a great deal that is very French about New Orleans, but then nearby one could walk up steps to the Mississippi and watch the one remaining paddle steamer, the Natchez, with its tall thin black funnels, tying up at the wharf, and with the strident sounds of jazz issuing out of the buildings in the streets, it is also very American. The enormous quantity of double cast iron verandas on two floors, supported by long thin pillars to the pavement gave the narrow streets of the old quarter a unique quality completely its own.

On the opposite side of the square to the café was a museum and outside it a very interesting early submarine. It could not have held more than one or possibly two people.

Returning one day to the hotel, I saw a black taxi driver in his cab outside teaching himself to play the banjo he agreed to take me the next evening to the airport, I suggested 8.30, and was somewhat taken aback when he said he would be there at 7.30, so that he would not be late! Any way he was as good as his word, arriving in good time and giving me a conducted tour on the way. So there I was taking off from New Orleans into a black night sky, watching "On Golden Pond" high above the sea, and getting all of two hours sleep before being wakened for breakfast. Discovering the New World had been a wonderful experience."

Travelling in Europe with American Blacksmiths 1997.

At the end of August and through September of 1997, I made a 2000-mile journey through parts of Bavaria, Switzerland. Italy and Austria, with a group of 32 American blacksmiths on a tour organised by the Artist Blacksmith Association of North America. Our main purpose was to visit some nine blacksmith's workshops covering a wide range of technology, both old and new; two were still using tilt hammers worked by water wheels, while others were using some very modern machinery, photographic etching processes and computer enhanced drawings to produce designs and models for their ironwork. We also went to five museums and two major exhibitions of modern ironwork.

I met them in Munich and the first day we settled into the picturesque Gasthof Huber in Oberndorf, and after a "Welcome Dinner" we had a talk by Manfred Bergmeister, famous ironmaster, on his work in Germany and overseas.

Next morning we boarded our bus for Munich and he took us on a guided tour of the Cathedral for which he had made 23 great screens. I remember also his workshop and its many models, some were only a few inches long (as one might doodle on the back of an envelope), while others were up to size, often several for one work. After the Cathedral we visited the well-known Town Hall where, at noon, we watched the moving figures on the tower.

In the afternoon we left for a typical village blacksmith shop run as a family enterprise in Sonthofen.

Next day we crossed Lake Constance to Friedrichshafen in Germany, where the new Zeppelin Museum contains the reconstruction of a 108ft long section of the legendary LZ 129, the "Hindenburg". Visitors can climb aboard the retractable stairway and stroll past the authentically furnished passenger lounge and crew rooms. The tubular and leather armchairs must have seemed as stunningly part of a new world as the whole concept of airship travel, comparable only with the space age of today. It was quite realistic as one gazed down through angled viewing windows to television screens below, showing the scuttling figures of ground crew casting off ropes and becoming smaller and smaller as we seemed to rise into the air.

The illusion of travelling by Zeppelin is followed by subsequent exhibits allowing insights into the history and technology of airship aviation. The airships of Count Zeppelin (1838 - 1917) were the cradle for entire branches of industry, aeroplanes from Dornier, engines from Maybach, gearboxes from ZF. All these companies emerged out of the "technology transfer" of airship construction. On the ground floor there was an enormous and superb Zeppelin car.

There was a fine exhibition of modern ironwork at Friedrichshafen and many pieces displayed in the grounds around the exhibition hall. Anthony Robinson's Auferstehung still stands proudly overlooking the lake but his new swirling crucifix was placed so far at a distance that it was difficult to get anywhere near unless one could find the time for an extra half-hour walk.

The next day was a Sunday and we visited the Iron Library in the Paradise Convent very near Schaffhausen. More accurately this is a library relative to all metals. It is housed in beautiful old buildings completed in 1602, the earliest being the gatehouse dating from 1268. The estate was purchased in 1918 by George Fischer head of a world-wide industrial partnership, which now have some 12,000 employees. They produce piping systems, castings, swivel bearings, engine and transmission components, and various types of cast iron and aluminium. The manufacturing technology department specialises in plant engineering, producing plant for the plastic and foundry industries.

The library contains some 37,000 units. Users who come to study from a distance are even able to arrange to stay on the premises. Outside are displayed a shining Pelton wheel turbine, which I believe they continued to make until 1953, and an anvil of 1789.

Some wonderful books were laid out for us to see - a first edition of Georgius Agricola's "De Re Metallica", Ramelli's "Mechanical Inventions", books by Réaumure, Isaac Newton, Otto von Guericke, inventor of the air vacuum, of Robert Boyle and Mons. Papin, and among later volumes " La Tour de Trois Cents Metres", the building construction of the Eiffel Tower. On the open shelves I noticed the "Diaries of Lady Charlotte Guest" and books on Naysmyth, Gilchrist Thomas and Telford. It was like being offered a great feast and then being given no time to eat anything!

On September 1st we boarded the bus to the Tuggenburger Blacksmith Workshop and Museum where the owner and his wife still carry on working metal in the modern industrial age. He demonstrated the making of an axe head, a skill passed down from his father. In the afternoon we drove to Christ of Friedrich's shop in Sennwald. Here he had restored the old water wheel and its drop hammer so the smiths were able to experience working at a water-wheel hammer. In the evening at supper we sat at long tables in wonderful surroundings outside the forge with mountains all around us.

Next day at Bruncio after a stop at a blacksmith's shop we went to the South Tyrolean open-air museum in a mountainous region.

Between Bruncio and Stia we stayed at a religious boarding house, run by nuns, half way up a mountain. It was so clean that one could have eaten one's meals off the floor, but one of the blacksmiths after taking a bath in a bathroom next to my bedroom, was standing on the bath mat when he saw one corner of it moving suspiciously and found a black scorpion underneath. Fortunately he was a blacksmith from Arizona who knew just what to do, he squirted it with bottled soap, and next morning at breakfast was carrying the body around in a match box.

Next day we drove a long way to Feltre to visit the Rizzarda Museum with much fine ironwork. On September the 4th we attended the opening of the "Biennale di Arte Fabbrile" in Stia. It is an attractive Italian hill town, some 50km from both Florence and Arezzo. The Festival really divides into two parts, there is an exhibition of modern ironwork in a park, where smiths can create their own entries at a line of hearths set up down one side. This year the competition was being held as a memorial to Antonio Benetton who died in 1996.

Everyone was there, I found Craig Knowles who had trudged into town the night before carrying his heavy iron candlestick entry and all his camping gear on his back. I saw a group of iron sculptures by Mauro Bortollotti near the exhibition park that impressed me immensely. There were figures for a nativity group, a standing figure and a pregnant seated woman and a mounted Don Quixote, he welds his pieces of shaped forged iron together leaving the welded seam to give a pleasing texture that helps to define the folds of a garment; these memorable figures have grace and strength in equal measure.

The Arno runs through the town and on the other side of the river many booths have been set up down through the centre of Tanucci Square, an old and beautifully arcaded street. These were to house trade stands, and it seems as if this was where the Italians had the edge over us all. They had found a way of really bringing ironwork to the people. There were smithing firms from all over Italy and the place was crowded. Farmers and smiths had come in from the country and urban Italians jostled through the booths all day.

There was a vast amount of ironwork, the traditional outweighing the modern. On the stand of Enzo Caporali there were some very elegant modern designs, which were all simple but somehow reminiscent of medieval times. It was interesting to see here an old technique used in a modern manner. Later in the tour we visited the Hofkirk in Innsbruck where there is an iron grill round the tomb of Maximilian. It is formed of traditional German 'rope' work and has shields of flat plate painted in colours, and larger pieces on which cherubs are exquisitely painted to give a three dimensional effect. Caporali had used the same idea, where two beautifully painted affronted lions formed the main feature of the headboard of an iron bed. It seems Italians have never stopped making iron bedsteads, and they were to be seen inspired by every historical period as well as modern designs. In one, large pieces of coloured glass were clasped in claw settings.

We must have visited Florence during our stay in Stia where we were allowed to see the Cultural Ministry Restoration Laboratory. Here we saw one of the famous "Paradise" doors from the Baptistry. held horizontally on a trestle, and nearby two of the gilded bronze panels by Ghiberti normally attached to it. These were in glass cases packed with silica gel. The doors were damaged in the floods of 1966, but long exposure to the air especially with modern pollutants, has been a greater cause of deterioration. Professor Morini described how the gilding had been lifted by a film of copper corrosion, oxides and other salts, and the difficulties involved in stabilising the problem.

Upstairs in the jewellery department we met Signor Pieri Giorgio who showed us two 18th century reliquaries of silver and a 15th century cross with a base of copper and wood covered with gold and mercury amalgam. Much of the background was blue enamel and Signor Giorgio described the process of restoration, which had to date taken nine months. Throughout, the point was made that in Renaissance times artisan workshops with masters and apprentices working together were able to hand down the necessary skills, and that now although we have the skills we do not have the experience, because the continuity has been broken. A very high standard of technology is being used to study and restore the objects, and absolutely no metal is being removed, which was necessary until the comparatively recent past.

It was also while we were at Stia that we made a trip into the valley of Casentino to see two castles, wonderful Tuscan countryside in the Apennines, a region dominated by castles and Romanesque churches. In the evening we enjoyed a celebration dinner of Tuscan specialities.

On September 8th we began to drive north towards Venice and this must have been when we stopped at Pomposa Abbey. I have found myself at Pomposa more than once and there is so much to see in this fascinating building. There is an early mosaic floor, of 1226, masses of frescoes and the great bell tower. Perhaps the most memorable, because they are so unusual, are the ceramic bowls, let decoratively into the facade of the abbey along with Byzantine carvings of animals and birds.

We did not stay in Venice itself but in Mestre, and we had two glorious sunny days in which to see what is surely the most beautiful city in the world. I could hardly believe that it was forty years since I had spent a single day there with Ron; how could I have left it so long before returning? In future I should go there whenever I could, and would certainly have three full weeks there in the years to come. If one grows tired of walking along beside the canals and down the narrow streets, then it is just as delightful to ride on the vaporetto down the Grand Canal and give your feet a rest. I love the great bronze doors on San Marco with their rows of lion-head knockers, the way the four bronze horses above seem set to stride out across the square. On the second afternoon we took a boat to the island of San Servolo to visit UNESCO'S European Architectural Heritage centre for training craftsmen, which included wrought ironwork.

We stayed a night in Treviso to visit the Simon Benetton studio and the Toni Benetton Museum. Antonio and his son Simon, are undoubtedly the great artist blacksmiths of modern day Italy. The museum is in a beautiful old villa in Marocco di Mogliano and one can study his work from its early beginnings to its end. Toni was first a well known sculptor who in later life took to forged iron work. He was born in Treviso in 1910 and studied with Arturo Martini at the Venice Academy of Art.

He had exhibitions in Trieste and Treviso, and in later years in Milan, Tokyo, Bologna, London and Canada.

On Sept 11th we visited the Di Maser Winery for a wine tasting. We had completed the wine tasting and were sitting waiting about for some time, so I went to our leader and said could I just pop down the road to look at the Palladian chapel for a few minutes. I was not long so it was with considerable surprise that when I returned I saw the coach disappearing down the road. So here I was in some remote and unknown part of Italy; I set off purposefully down the middle of the road, hoping it would not be too long before they realised that I was not with them. After a while two little figures appeared on the horizon and I was rescued.

As we went north into Austria we visited the State School for Metal Trades in Innsbruck, with a display of some very fine metalwork. Then we went to a Bell Casting Foundry and Museum Next day, with a while for "last minute shopping" and a farewell dinner, we set off the day after for Munich Airport.

I Returned to Venice in 1998.

Having briefly been in Venice for a couple of days with the Americans I could not believe that I had left it forty years since I had returned after the day there with Ron, and I was determined to see more of it as soon as I could.

At the end of September 1998 I arranged to go there with an old school friend, but shortly before we were due to leave she fell down and broke her ankle and was unable to come. Geoff Willetts, a friend I had met some years before on a holiday looking at stately homes, and as his partner had recently died I asked him if he would like to join me; This he did and we left Heathrow on September 27th, flying to Marco Polo Airport. On arrival one can take a bus to the coach station, next to the railway station on the Grand Canal. From there it is a simple matter to take a vaporetto to the Hotel Ala. The hotel is only a few yards through a narrow alleyway that opens out into a square, from the vaporetto stop "Giglio", which makes it very convenient.

From the hotel one can walk to the wooden bridge Accademia across the canal or through a maze of streets towards San Marco. On the first day we took a vaporetto to Zaccaria and then to the Fontamenti le Nuova on the other side of the island. This was interesting because the boat took us past the elaborate entrance, between two tall towers, to the Arsenal itself, where the ships used to be built, past shipyards and rope walks. From the Fontemente de Nuova one could look across to the funeral island of S. Michele where Venetians are laid to rest. We walked along the front and turned left to the Jesuit church of Chiesa di Santa Maria Assunta detta I Gesuita, a wonderful place with marble walls like damask.

We followed pointers printed on walls to Ca d'oro, known as the golden house because it was built between 1420 and 1434 and at that time had polychrome and gilded decoration. Full of treasures and from the first floor balcony one can look down to the arcade of the fish market; on the corners of the balcony sit little stone lions.

That evening we tried eating at the Café Raffaele, at the back of the hotel where one can eat at tables overlooking a canal and watch gondolas pass, sometimes with singing and music.

Next day we took the vaporetto to the island of Torcello. One walks along the side of the canal from the landing place to a group of buildings and the Cathedral and its bell tower and the round church of Santa Fosca. It is a wonderfully peaceful and evocative spot. The nearby museum contains remains from at least ten churches that were once on Torcello, when the island had some 20,000 inhabitants, including a magnificent 11th century wall fresco of the Last Judgement.

Next day we crossed the Accademia Bridge to the quiet district of Dorsoduro, visited two churches and lunched in a square with some trees.

One evening we went to a concert in a church, memorable not so much for the music but that the fire alarms kept going off. The first time it looked as if we should be ushered out of the exits but after a few more times no one took any notice.

We found we enjoyed dining at the Ristorante Fiaschetta. Take the road straight ahead on the left of the statue of Goldoni in Camp San Bortolo, cross the canal at the end, and continue until you see the restaurant on the left.

The weather was not very good but we enjoyed the week very much anyway.

To Europe with American Blacksmiths in 1999.

For three weeks in August-September 1999, I again went with American blacksmiths of ABANA to Europe. These excellent trips of the Artist Blacksmiths of North America were organised and led by Leonard Masters. This time we travelled through parts of Germany, the Czech Republic and Austria; it included the Annual Czech Blacksmith Hefaiston Conference held in Helfstyn Castle with many demonstrations and exhibitions. We journeyed through Berlin, Dresden, Prague, Vienna, Weyer Markt and Salzburg. I met them in Berlin, Achim and Helga Kuhn joined us, and on August 20th we all went to the Pergamon Museum. This contains a reconstruction of the great Pergamon Altar, originally built around 170 BC, on what is now the west coast of Turkey, opposite Lesbos. The ancient city was discovered in 1878 and later excavated under the direction of Carl Humann. The great flight of steps and colonnade was surrounded by a considerable frieze of carvings of battles between gods and giants. Part of the altar has been reconstructed and more than a hundred of the over-lifesize figures on slabs are shown in the museum.

We went on a tour of Berlin and saw the Brandenburg gate; Achim had restored the statues on the top.

The afternoon was free and I walked round a Berlin street market with Peter Happny and Tom Yeager. It stood between two churches, a modern church and the ruins of an old one. We had a great time, eating ice cream and strawberries, and I found a stall kept by a North American Indian selling silver and turquoise jewellery. I bought a long necklace of turquoise chips with a pendant of labradorite.

Next morning we left at 8 a.m. sharp for Dresden via Meissen. As one nears the City of Meissen one passes the Gothic castle of Albrechtsburg perched on a precipitous craggy outcrop. It was here that the porcelain was originally made when the process was still a secret. We proceeded to the porcelain factory where we learnt about the production, with demonstrations, and admired the exquisite fine china.

We saw the outside of the Pillnitz Palace, and as I wandered round the grounds, I heard someone playing what sounded like panpipes. Perhaps it was because it was so unexpected but it felt as if the sound might have been coming from fairyland.

What I remember most about Dresden was the photographs in stands outside postcard shops, showing the city in ruins after we had bombed it. I was horrified, I know we have often been blamed for this action but I heard later (for we knew little of these things at the time), how the Germans had bombed Coventry, it was the first and worst night of bombing that they received, when hundreds of 'planes crossed the city in one direction dropping bombs, then another wave of bombers crossed in the opposite direction destroying most of the city centre. It was the origin of saturation bombing, reducing a town to ruins. I heard many years later a senior high-ranking officer of the R.A.F. say "they taught us how to do it".

Next day we visited the great wall of Meissen tiles showing the Procession of Dukes, a number of restored ironwork gates and Christ Church in Strehlen, then had a demonstration by Alfred Habermann. The evening was "free" and this usually meant that one fell exhausted into a chair for a good rest.

By August 24th we had reached Prague and were advised to put on stout walking shoes. The coach took us to Hradcany Castle and then we walked to the Charles Bridge. I remember the great wide river and looking down on delightful houses. We went to the Old Town Square and the Astronomical clock built in 1410, then more blacksmiths workshops and tool-making demonstrations.

Next day we visited a locomotive factory in the rain. Later we went to the workshop of Leopold Habermann junr. Then in Olomouc, Moravia's oldest town, to visit another workshop, then boarded the coach for Prerov.

The day after, we left at 9 a.m. for the Annual Czech Blacksmith Conference at Helfstyn Castle. The castle is one of the most extensive in Europe in which there was a fine ironwork exhibition of modern ironwork. There was also a reconstruction of a working Trebuchet or machine, more than 17m high, for slinging heavy stones. This was a type in use from the 13th century until their function was displaced by artillery.

On Aug. 30th we boarded the bus for Vienna. The first day was spent sight-seeing and I will remember St. Stephen's Cathedral with its jazzy patterned roof and the horse drawn carriages waiting round it.

The next day we actually had some free time and it gave me the opportunity to make two excursions on my own. I had long wanted to see the white Lipizzaner horses and as there seemed to be no official performance while we were there I made my way to the Spanish Riding School where one could buy a ticket for what I suppose was a kind of training session or rehearsal. It was a magnificent room with enormous chandeliers and had a balcony with seating all round. I sat entranced and enjoyed every minute of it. The Spanish Riding School in Vienna has cultivated classical horsemanship for over four hundred years and demonstrates the haute école of horsemanship as practised by the Viennese Royal Court.

The other thing I was anxious to do in Vienna was to see the inside of the Opera House and accordingly set off in a taxi one evening to see a performance of Verdi's Ernani. I sat in a box with other people and was very impressed, not only by the opera but also by the auditorium, the staircases and various opulent rooms.

On September 2nd we reached Graz where one finds the Hanns Schell Collection, one of the finest private collections of locks and treasure chests in Europe. The exhibits range from African wooden door latches, bolts to metal locks and caskets of incredibly fine workmanship and great beauty.

Also in Graz there is the Armoury, the people of Graz, in the Styrian area of Austria, had a strong proprietary feeling for their Armoury. On the border of the Holy Roman Empire they felt bound in honour to protect the Empire and the whole culture of the Occident from the menace of the Turks. Rushing forwards towards Europe the Turks had conquered Constantinople in 1453. When Belgrade fell to them in 1521 and Hungary lost her independence five years later their security was threatened for the next 200 years. In 1480 there were about 20,000 Turks roving central and southern Styria. It was necessary to keep a sufficient stock of arms and ammunition always ready for use.

Today there remains some 32,000 pieces of the original arms and armour, though there were once many more. After around 1700 the danger of the Turks ended and the defence was taken over by the State. Marie Theresa wanted to take the armoury to Vienna but the people would not part with it and diplomatically asked the Empress to allow them to keep it as a monument to Styrian bravery. This request was granted and is why it remains the only armoury in the world to be preserved almost in its entirety. During the last war it was jealously guarded and secreted from the Russians in numerous castles in the country.

In the 16th century the arms were stored in a nearby loft in the Herrengrasse, with the heavy guns in the arsenal huts. However, in 1642 the armoury building was begun and completed in two years. To climb the stone steps up one floor after another and see the wooden racks closely packed with arms and armour is a most impressive experience. One is overwhelmed by the sheer quantity; every inch is utilised, with small objects, like powder horns, hung in rows on the ceilings. The 32,000 arms include more than 3300 armours, breastplates and helmets, and more than 7800 small arms. For the most part they are the weapons of war for simple soldiers, and as such are perhaps more evocative than the more elaborately displayed exhibits in many museums. One can almost hear the call to arms, the hustle and bustle of passing out the arms with the enemy almost at the gate.

There can be few areas more rewarding to those interested in metallurgy than a visit to the Styrian Iron Road in Austria. From Linz to Leoben one can trace a thousand years of Iron mining and working. The Iron Mountain at Erzberg has been giving up its ore since the early middle ages, and today it is the largest iron-ore surface mine in central Europe. The iron ore is siderite and contains an average of 30 to 35% iron, about 2% manganese, and only very small amounts of unwanted phosphorus and sulphur. Underground mining has not taken place here since 1986, when it became no longer viable. Open cast mining, however, takes place on the terraces where the lower deposit outcrops face the town of Eisenberg. One can board a 5-ton truck and "ride the Hauly" snaking along the twisting open cast terraces up the mountain. It is an impressive journey, the air grows cold as one rises towards the top, and looking far below a little blue lake can be seen at the lowest level. The ore is crushed here to a diameter of 10cm and transported to Leoben or Donawitz.

A few miles from the Iron Mountain lies the little town of Vordernberg that was once full of iron master's houses and their Stuckofen or high furnaces for smelting the iron ore. In earlier times there were no less than ten furnaces in the narrow valley and today there are still the remains of several. They smelted by the direct method, the bloomery furnaces of the early middle ages began to be driven in the 13th century by water power. So long as the countryside was full of timber and the product required was wrought iron there was little incentive to go over to the blast furnace. By about 1760, however, most of the furnaces were the High Shaft or High Stophen Furnaces, but few were the true blast furnace until the mid 19th century. Radwerk 10 is visible from the main road on the outskirts of Vordernberg. While from the main square of the town, with its decorative wrought iron well head of 1668 can be seen the large red stone building that is a mid 19th century blast furnace and is now the home of the Ironwork Museum. It is quite unlike any remains we have in Britain, the stack is surrounded by a three-story building, and rises from the centre of the roof in a bizarre fashion. Wagons and rails brought in the ore to the building on a level with the charging floor, and in later days was roasted in the actual building, a bank of ovens still remain.

That night we stayed in the attractive little town of Weyer Markt and made a number of visits in the area, a nail maker in Losenstein, Scythe makers in Laussa and Derulschfeistritz, a pocket-knife maker in Trattaibach and an armourer in Molin. Here Johann Schmidberger, and his sons, still make traditional armour and armaments, including fine swords, in a smithy that dates back to 1350.

We left Weyer Markt for Salzburg where I was able to see a performance by the renowned Salzburger Marionetten Theatre. In Stiegkeller we had a farewell dinner, where the dining room staff were mystified by so many men with beards, and asked if they were priests! The next day we were in Munich Airport to part and go our separate ways.

Entering a New Century and Travelling in Europe with the Friends of the Museum 2001.

It was in 2001 that the terrible disaster happened in the United States of America. I hardly ever watch television in the afternoon but on September 11th there was an old black and white film with Laurence Olivier as Nelson and I thought I should like to see it again. Half way through the news broke in, and I watched with mounting horror all that was happening in New York for the rest of the afternoon, To see the two aeroplanes flying into the great tower, to see people running away, to watch the flames and the clouds of smoke was appalling. In later news bulletins one saw people actually throwing themselves out of the windows as the highest floors collapsed. I have never seen anything so terrible. The sympathy and "togetherness" was universal. Even before we knew that we had lost 200 British people in the disaster we were practically singing the National Anthem of the States with our hands on our hearts! The Queen attended St. Paul's for a memorial service and we had three minutes silence then and in church on several occasions.

I had long been a member of the Friends of the Cheltenham Art Gallery and Museum and they ran trips abroad led by Jenny and Douglas Ogle. In the Autumn of 2001 I joined them for a study tour of the west borderlands of Germany. Although their tours included old buildings and churches they also took in modern art and architecture. So it was that six days after the disaster I boarded a plane for Frankfurt, none too happily I might say, for an autumn study tour. It was a varied and unusual trip.

We went first to Saarbrucken and walked round the old town with its splendid Baroque buildings and 18th century townscape and the attractive St. Johanner Markt; and marvelled at the white organ with 4000 pipes in the Ludwigskirche. Outside the Catholic Church of Sante John, I was particularly impressed by a modern bronze hand by Ernst Alt holding a 'rope' handrail that led to bronze doors.

The day after the coach took us through the vineyards of the Mosel Valley to the picturesque small wine producing town of Bernkastel. There was a most elaborate bronze fountain with many figures and great bunches of grapes amid black and white half-timbered houses.

The day following Riquewihr was an even more attractive wine village, its half-timbered houses hung with flower filled hanging baskets, where one could look out on to vineyard covered hills.

We continued to Trier. I found Trier a most exciting place, one was familiar from photographs with the Porta Negra, the Roman Black Gates, but nothing had prepared me for the size of them, they seemed to dwarf the town. Some stones weigh as much a two tons each and in later years the rounded end of the building would become an early Christian church. We also looked at a very interesting Basilica type building erected by the Emperor Constantine, architecturally very plain and now used as a church. It was in complete contrast with the next building round the corner, the Electoral Palace all elaborate pink and white, topped with statues and fronted with Sphinxes with elegant women's heads and hands that were great paws.

Next day we journeyed to Colmar. It was incredibly picturesque, half-timbered houses with steeply pitched roofs, strung out along each side of the river. There were hanging baskets and flowers in containers along the edge.

We went to see Belfont a town with 17th century fortifications where we visited a gallery of modern art. Then, for me one of the highlights of the trip, a visit to Ronchamp, opened in 1955, to see Corbusier's masterpiece, the church of Notre Dame du Haut. It is a small church, modern, very modern, but built for pilgrims so that there was a pulpit outside and room for a very large congregation in the open air. Inside the simple white walls were pierced with small windows with glass of intense blocks of bright colour - a most impressive place.

On the same day we went to Sacré Coeur church in Audincourt with its stained glass by Leger and a Baptistry that particularly appealed to me with glass all round glowing with lemon and orange colours by J. Brazine, made by J. Barillet.

The following day was also very special, a visit to the Vitra factory complex at Weil am Rhein, one incredible modern building after another, Frank Gehrey's Museum, Zaha Hadid's Fire Station and Tadao Ando's Conference Pavilion. The chair museum brought together a profusion of chairs, some of which remain firmly in the mind. The classic Thonet bent beech-wood chair surprisingly as early as 1859; the iconic Miles Van der Rohe steel frame of 1929, there are many more colourful chairs but few were as lasting and satisfying as these.

The trip was completed by journeying through the Black Forest to Freiberg where I particularly enjoyed the ironwork in the cathedral. There were 16th century wrought iron rails to several of the chapels in the apse. These were typically German employing the techniques of rope work, round section bar loosely bent while hot into knot-like forms. Several pieces of the bar are sometimes opened into "cages" as like as not forming parts of large flowers as finials. Another typical technique is that of flat cut-out sheet iron; often this is blank and it is only the silhouette that might tell what it was supposed to represent. At Freiberg, however, there are unexpected riches, what looks like the original paint remains on a railing of 1570; flat bunches of leaves are coloured in delicate greens, others over the entrance to an end chapel is an ornate cut-out of flat painted figures. This technique is seen at its most famous in the screen round the tomb of Maximilian I in Innsbruck, Austria, dated 1572, where cherubs as much a foot high inhabit the ironwork, combining the art of the iron-forger with that of the painter of trompe l'oeil.

We ended in Stuttgart with a modern art collection and walking round the old part of the city, where memorably we saw a beautifully decorated beer dray drawn by grey horses.

I had already gone with the Friends (in 1998) to Brussels and Rotterdam which enabled me among other things, to see the European Parliament Headquarters, and before that (1995) to The Hague, Haarlem and Amsterdam with them. I had already seen and enjoyed Amsterdam, with a friend Mike Grange, I find the high houses with their ornate gables along the canals very attractive. Along the Keizers and Prinsen canal boats often form a brightly coloured band or frieze below the house facades where one looks upwards to wooden stuttered windows that were once the store places of the city.

Number 605 Herengracht the Willet Holthuysen house was built in 1689 but although it is now a museum, it retains all the atmosphere of a private house, from the neat geometric parterres of the garden to the cherub strewn ceiling of the sitting room. Best of all the basement kitchen with tile pictures of birds in ornately delicate cages set in plain, so called white tiles of the 17th century, which are really all possible permutations of subtle pale blue, pinky beige and green.

Amsterdam is full of surprises, turn through a small arched doorway away from the busy market and cafés of Spui, into the Begijnhof and the centuries fall away. The quiet court has both a Presbyterian and a

Catholic church, and a 15th century wooden house, all set around with early gabled buildings, the Dutch equivalent of almshouses. Walk through the court to reach Amsterdam's Historisch Museum; how could one resist the temptation to enter, after the enticement of armour displayed behind glass to the open street ,and of automatic doors that lead one, all unsuspecting, into an art gallery of city burghers -the museum itself does not disappoint.

Some of my greatest personal enjoyments were the antique and old Delft tile shops in Nieuwe Spiegelstraat; the unusual and intricate ironwork on the Sheepvaarthuis (Prince Hendrick's Arcade), a building by J.M. Van de Meyos 1912, and the fantastic Art Deco Tuschinski Cinema in Reguliersbreestraat of 1921.

A rather unusual form of entertainment and feature of Amsterdam life was a peripatetic morning concert, which I made during a stay in the city with Mike. It was held in three churches, the players (of flute, viola and organ) and the audience, walking from one church to the next during each interval. We first walked through a rather sleazy part of the old city from Beursplein to Amstelkring, past drug-takers squatting trembling on filthy basement steps, and along narrow streets full of sex-shops. Once at the Museum Amstelkring, formerly a Catholic church, we were in a different world and sat surrounded by richly gilded treasures, oil paintings and triptychs, listening entranced to Telemann.

During the first interval the way to the Oude Kerk lay through the red light district. On each side of curving cobbled streets were narrow houses, each with an open door and an adjacent window revealing a bed and piles of cushions. Most, at this time of the morning, appeared deserted but in one of the first, two ample Negro women wore black fish-net tights and little else. Opposite a blonde in a brief bikini sat on a high stool like a statue; so reminiscent of an old Kodak advertising board that I was startled when she moved.

I also went to Barcelona with the "Friends". I had been there some years before but this visit gave me ample time to spend taking in the ironwork of Antonio Gaudi. I went for the first time to Güell Park; it is a fantastic riot of invention with ironwork and modern mosaic. Perhaps even more incredible is the roof of the Milà House

There are the imposing Dragon Gates at the entrance to the Güell Pavilions and elaborate arched doorways to the Güell Palace. Perhaps more restrained but no less superb are the gates and fence panels of Casa Vicens with their pattern of large and very realistic palm leaves.

Gaudi made alterations in 1904-06 to an old building in the Paseig de Gracia Barcelona, the Batllo House. Inside the stair-rails are typical Art Nouveau curves restrained but beautiful; outside numerous balconies have mask-like ironwork making it unique.

My favourite Gaudi building is the astonishing great curved wall of Casa Milà. It is a cliff-like facade made in 1906-12. The ironwork integrated into the sculptural building transcends Art Nouveau it is as modern in outlook as anything that has been made in recent years. The curving walls are complemented by ironwork balconies that form an integral part of the building design.

There are some thirty of these exterior balconies and all appear to be different; surely much of the detail must have been designed by the smiths themselves. The technique is that of cut plate forged into curvilinear forms and riveted together.

It is a stupendous concept who knows what was in the minds of those who created it a great troglodyte cliff whose ledges grow luxuriant plant forms, or a stone sea washing up succulent flat twisting ropes of seaweed, Where did Gaudi find his fantastic vision? He was not just ahead of this time, looking back now we can see that he was some hundred years before his time!

Surely no gates had been made like those on this building before, and from inside the courtyard one looks back to see their thick but curving shapes silhouetted against the outside light. The roof of the building has giant sculptures of menacing forms covered with large pieces of mosaic. It is surely the most impressive and unusual building in the world.

I sometimes went to London with the Friends usually to exhibitions and one such trip I remember well. Maybe the coach driver got a bit lost, perhaps we were going round in circles, we certainly crossed the river several times, but what an opportunity to see a succession of buildings from Lambeth Palace to the MI6 establishment. The mellow stone of the Houses of Parliament bathed in sunlight, Charles II's Chelsea Hospital, fleeting glimpses between the trees into the physic garden, and every so often some strangely coloured and shaped modern building squashed in between its more venerable neighbours. It had been some time since I had been on the South Bank so here was the new pedestrian footbridge and the great wheel of the London Eye, and a distant view of the Gherkin.

To see all this and a London crowd en fête. To see a performance in the Globe Theatre gave us an opportunity to know what an Elizabethan audience was really like, how like us they sweltered in the sun or presumably froze in the cold. I had been in the Swan at Stratford and did not expect the newly built Globe to be much different but it was. Here I really felt myself transported back in time the way the audience in the pit came and went and moved about, how pigeons flew down out of the sky, how the man behind me picked up every nuance of the bawdy humour, this was how Elizabethan audiences really were - no ghastly good taste here. I liked the obviously authentic bits of dance, the genuine musical instruments, and the rabid enthusiasm at the end.

I remember the 1951 Exhibition, the Skylon and the Dome and every man in a suit - I marvel how London reinvents itself through the years was it not Dr Johnson who said "When a man is tired on London he is tired of Life"!

It was on a later occasion we went to London with the Friends. I cannot remember where we went, some exhibition I expect, but I do recall that we had lunch in a café on Greenwich Common and afterwards walked across the common to visit some major house, It is the walk that I remember because it took in a fantastic view that made the day for me. On the right one could see Greenwich Observatory, straight ahead Canary Wharf and over to the left Greenwich Palace; I had visited all these places individually but to see them all in relation to each other, spread out in this way was a revelation.

In July 2005 I wrote to Lilo and Leonard (Masters) to tell them about a trip I had made to London.

"The week before last I went to London to adjudicate a very fine iron screen made by Jim Horrobin in memory of Sir Winston Churchill, in the crypt of St. Paul's Cathedral. We wanted to award it the Tonypandy trophy. I went on the coach, it is handy because it is only just around the corner from where I live, and as I am over 60 (well over!) I can go for half price, which makes it extraordinarily cheap, only £8 return. When I got to Victoria I decided to take a taxi to St. Paul's, it is many years since

I used a London taxi, and I found to my surprise that it cost me £14 - seems crazy when one compares the two prices. There were five of us from the British Artist Blacksmiths judging panel, and three officials from the Worshipful Company of Blacksmiths. We met the Treasurer of St. Paul's and it was very interesting to hear how they look forward for a number of years and how carefully they decide what sort of memorial they should have. The position was chosen because it is near the tombs of the Duke of Wellington (victor of Waterloo), and Admiral Lord Nelson (Trafalgar) -three great warriors together.

Afterwards we had a very good lunch at a city hostelry. One of the blacksmiths wrote to me the following week and I was much amused by one paragraph - "I have to say I found the Worshipful Company experience quite strange, but was most impressed by their ability to get through most of five bottles of wine in one lunchtime!" The Wardens of the Company, although they wear ties with hammers on, are not of course blacksmiths, but "something in the City". I got on very well with one of them sitting next to me, and he kindly lent me his chauffeur driven car to take me back to Victoria Coach Station.

Prince Charles was to have been married on April 8th, but owing to the Pope's funeral it had to be postponed until the 9th. I was very annoyed as I had kept the day free as it is my habit to watch such affairs on TV with a glass of something good to drink, but when it was moved to the Saturday, I had to be in Gloucester as President of the Gloucestershire Society for Industrial Archaeology by 9.30 to introduce delegates to a day of lectures. Fortunately I managed to get away after an early lunch and was back in time to see most of the ceremonies. I was glad it all went off well, and it was good to see him looking so happy as he does nowadays."

Northern Italy with the Bristol and Gloucester Archaeological Society 2000-2005.

Sometimes I took my holidays with the Bristol and Gloucester Archaeology Society. Their trips often included archaeological sites and were led by David Bartlett. I went with them in 2000 to Bologna and visited the Etruscan 6th to 4th century BC site at Marzabotto, thereafter there was a wealth of churches, abbeys and cathedrals. At the end of May we went south-east to Ravenna and on this occasion I had plenty of time to spend with all the wondrous mosaics. We can see into their Byzantine palaces where they knotted up the curtains out of the way, admire the mosaics as bright and colourful as the day they were put up. In San Vitale we can see the Emperor Justinian with a crown of gems and a great brooch on his shoulder. The courtiers and soldiers all standing on each other's feet in order to squash them into the space available. His empress Theodora, who had once been a dancer, is sumptuously gowned and covered with jewels.

In the apse a young and beardless Christ, as he was depicted in the early years of Christianity, sits on the Universe. In the dome of the Arian Baptistry, of the 6th century, he stands naked in the river Jordan, baptised by John the Baptist who stands on the side of the river, while the God of the River sits on a rock on the other side, crowned with lobster claws on his head. It is so interesting to see a time when the Christian Church had no compunction in remembering the pagan gods from which it had sprung.

I loved the quiet restfulness of S. Apollinaire Nuovo with its long processions of virgins and martyrs, and enjoyed the depiction of Theodoric's Palace with its knotted curtains, and the glimpses over the wall of Classe so that we can see into the town behind.

In the Mausoleum of Galla Placidia, who had such an eventful life, we see again the young beardless Christ, this time as a shepherd, with a cross, amongst his sheep, beneath a vault of stars.

Northwards to the superb Italian gardens of the Villa Barbarigo and then to the burial place of Pretrarch, and Montagnana with almost intact medieval walls 15 to 17 metres high. One place that particularly stays in the mind was the picturesque hill of Monselice with seven little chapels all the way up on ones left.

Then several days in Ferrara, many things to see specially the Palace of Schifanoia with its Renaissance frescoes of the months. Handsome beautifully dressed young people, chariots pulled by swans, strange dragon-like birds, monkeys or even horses.

I went with them also in 2005 and stayed some days in Trento driving out to a small number of places and visiting castles; Castello di Drena, Castel Roncolo, Castel Ivano, and Castello del Buonconsiglio with wonderful medieval frescoes of the seasons.

Underneath the modern city of Trento we saw the remains of Roman Tridentum. Another day we went to see what still remains of a prehistoric bronze age lake village near Fiavè. There were still wooden stakes in the water and what amazed me was that they were sprouting leaves. I should have thought that after so long the wood would be dead. On the shores of Lake Molveno we visited an ancient Venetian water powered saw-mill. The scenery was wonderful, we were often in sight of the Dolomites, and spent one afternoon driving through most spectacular mountains and up into mountain pastures full of wild flowers.

I very much enjoyed the 8th century St, Proculo at Naturno, where a fresco shows the saint flying through the air escaping from the town walls and a small frescoed church in the middle of a farmyard, though I cannot remember where.

We went north to the Abbey of Novacella Bressanone and then to Bolzano to the Archaeological Museum. I found this the most interesting part of the journey. We were able to see the body of the iceman preserved in a glacier for some 5000 years or more. In September 1991 Ericka and Helmut Simon were taking their holiday in the Italian South Tyrol; they were experienced mountaineers and were climbing the Similaun summit on the Otztal Alps. Becoming benighted they decided next day, by then the 19th of September, to climb the 3514 metre Fineilspitze and during the descent they discovered the upper part of a man's body sticking out of the glacier. They imagined it to be the body of a climber lost perhaps twenty or thirty years before, and the police were informed.

Shortly after the body, and various objects that were scattered around, were collected by a helicopter. Gradually it became established that the body dated from the Neolithic or early Copper Age. He was carrying flint implements including a flint dagger, a bow of yew wood and arrow shafts. There were two birch-bark containers and most important of all a copper axe set in a wooden haft held in position with leather or skin binding. The cast copper axe head was 9.3 centimetres long and carefully honed to a sharp edge. The ore from which it was made is thought to be from the surface. It is the only prehistoric axe preserved complete with haft, blade and binding.

It is thought that the man was a shepherd and his clothing seemed to have consisted of a cap, an upper garment of fur, a pair of leggings covering calf and thigh, and a loincloth, a pair of shoes and a cloak of plaited grass.

The discovery and preservation of the Iceman has been carefully described by Konrad Splindler. "The Man in the Ice", by Konrad Splindler. Weidenfeld and Nicholson, London. 1994.

Amina at home

In Venice with Ivan 2002.

In August 2002 I flew to Rome to stay with Ivan. He had always been a Catholic and in recent years he had become a priest with the White Fathers. They were founded in 1868 in Algeria by Cardinal Lavigerie and in those days wore a white habit and a black burnous. It was a dangerous business then and a number of them were killed when they ventured into the interior. At first Ivan worked in Burkina Faso for some years, then the archivist to the order died and he was asked if he would become archivist at the headquarters in Rome. He was obviously the best qualified so he felt obliged to comply, So it was that I made my way to a big house in the Via Aurelia which looked down on Rome, St. Peter's and the Janiculum Hill. It was built some sixty years ago for until then they had headquarters in North Africa, there is a very fine commemorative hanging in the crypt of the chapel to the twenty-two martyrs of Uganda. In the late 19th century these Ugandans were burnt alive by their king for adhering to the Christian faith.

Normally there were about forty fathers in residence and usually some students, but being August there were seldom more than twenty of us sat down to a meal.

We spent several very pleasant days in Rome when we visited the Museo Nazionale Romano where I especially enjoyed the Roman wall paintings from the Villa Farnesina and the Gardens of Livia that had inspired the wall paintings I had made in my bathroom many years before. Some unusual exhibits were bronze lion and wolf heads from two whole boats from a lake that Caligula had used for parties.

In the afternoon I rested in the garden and in the evening we went to a particularly good ice-cream shop that Ivan knew of in a little street near the Piazza Navona.

We went to St. Peter's and wandered through the Bernini Arcade, which I always find so impressive. One of the delights of being in Rome with Ivan was that if he was wearing what he called "his clericals", when we entered the Vatican the Swiss Guards presented arms to us. They are so magnificent in their orange and blue uniforms that this is a very satisfying experience!

We went through to reach the catacombs under St. Peter's. It is like narrow streets from which rooms open off. In the rooms there are recesses where the bodies were placed and sometimes paintings on the walls, and the occasional mosaic on the floor. These are the earliest of the Christian burial places, between the 2nd and 4th centuries, and this is reflected by the subjects of the paintings. Often they are of shepherds and sheep which might equally be pagan scenes or illustrate the Bible. There are paintings depicting funeral feasts which could be the Last Supper, they are ambivalent, they do not too strongly commit themselves, they might equally be pagan or Christian scenes..

We went to the Borghese Gallery, not only oil paintings and statues but wonderful early rooms with painted walls and ceilings, putti, with golden garlands over the doors. Exquisitely patterned marbles, sometimes narrow panels over the doors with very Roman type paintings of tiny garlands of fruit and ribbons and little Roman-like heads in the centre. In the grounds, covered with pine trees, there are Cicadas singing.

Once when Ivan was busy I ventured into the centre by bus, when I wanted to get off I hesitated for the doors to open and before I could organise myself and my stick to descend they started to close again. I think everyone in the bus shouted to the driver to let me off, it was not necessary for me to say anything. I went to the Vatican Museum, full of magnificent carvings of sarcophagi and several interesting Bernard Buffet religious paintings in the modern section.

After a few days we caught the train to Venice, it was quite a long journey. When we arrived the station is next to the buses and it was quite easy to walk down the wide steps to the Vaporetto stop on the canal below.

We stayed at the Hotel Ala as I had done before, and started a wonderful week in Venice. I did not know it then but it was probably the last holiday I should spend with Ivan. So long as he was in Europe we would meet up occasionally but a few years later he retired, and returned to his birth place, Australia.

I never tired of sitting in the Vaporetto and looking at the buildings on each side of the canal. There was colour everywhere, on the boats, on the houses, it was an always moving panorama of delight.

On Monday we went to the Rezzonico Museum exquisite interiors and a fine collection of 18th century art. I particularly enjoyed the paintings of Venice by Ciardi though they were comparatively modern. We went round the church of the Carmini with its Tiepolos and the enormous church of Santa Maria Gloriosa dei Frari. We then took a protracted lunch in the Campo Santa Margarita, not going back to the hotel until about half past five, then in the evening to my favourite restaurant Fiaschetteria Tosana, for a very good mushroom sauce with duck breast followed by Tiramisa, wandering home about half past ten.

The next day we had intended going to the island of Torcello but the boats were on strike, so we walked to the Arsenal. It was built in the year 1104 but added to later. There was quite a nice little café near the entrance. We sat at a little table in the open drinking white wine while admiring the impressive lions on each side of the gates; they were brought from Greece by Morosini in 1607. The two smaller lions added in 1718, after the relief of Corfu may have come originally from the Lion Terrace on Delos.

A long walk over to Campo Giovanni e Paolo with the impressive bronze statue of Colleoni, and somewhere had king prawns in spaghetti followed by little biscuits to dip in sweet white wine.

The following day the boats were running and we took a long trip to Torcello, calling at the Lido, Burano and Murano. It was a hot day but there was a pleasant breeze blowing and I even put on my silk cardigan. We went first to look at the Basilica, then found more restaurants, and had an excellent lunch; I had an enormous plate of mussels and scallops and Ivan had mixed sea food with black pasta. We seemed to be having an eating day and I followed my first course with veal escallops, ham and melted cheese and Ivan opted for mixed fried fish. I had completely fallen for Tiramisa but it often seems not as good in Italy as it is at home; they do not seem to use enough cream. We returned to Santa Fosca and when we had gone round we went to the museum. After resting at the hotel we walked in the direction of the Fenice Theatre but it had been badly burnt some time before and it was covered with scaffolding and with a sign saying it would be complete in 470 days!

We were looking to have an ice-cream but the streets in this area seemed narrow and poverty stricken so we settled for seeing San Marco and the Doge's Palace which looked magnificent by night. We were doing things that I had never done before in Venice and ended up sitting under the arcade in Saint Mark's Square eating an expensive ice-cream and listening to a trio "I took one look at you, that's all I meant to do, and then my heart stood still" - that kind of music. There was a motley crew walking along the arcade, all rather surrealist; nearby two small children with their parents sat listening to the trio. The smallest little boy, sitting cross-legged on his chair, never took his eyes off the players - as good as gold, it was obviously a great treat. Walked home, lots going on, people, music - Venice by night.

Thursday we took the Vaporetto to the Academia Bridge to go to the Academia Art Gallery then walked to Zattere allo Spirito and lunched at a little restaurant hidden in a corner, nice and cool at al Gondolieri between the Academia and the Guggenheim. I really liked the place. We seemed to be into our stride now three excellent courses and a bottle of red wine.

On Friday we took the Vaporetto, a more direct route than when we went to Torcello, to Burano from San Marco front. It was an attractive place full of shops selling glass, but we eventually found a small shop selling beads there were beads from floor to ceiling in boxes on shelves. There were a number of people in the very small shop, think all the other customers were as entranced as I was what a happy hunting ground! Ivan opted to wait outside. I am afraid I kept him waiting half an hour, but he sheltered in the cool of an arcade and said his prayers. That is one of the good things about a priest he is always happy to say his prayers! I bought three-quarter inch amethysts the size of marbles and the same size rough corals, and some other disc shaped ones, and several rough turquoise. Later I strung them into a necklace I called "the Celtic princess necklace" because the varying sizes and substances gave them a very archaic look. The shop was not far from the Glass Museum on Font Cavour, after walking round it we had lunch and then went to Santa Maria e San Donato. This is a beautiful building, a blend of Byzantine and Lombard styles, rebuilt around 1140. The mosaic floor is one of the finest I have ever seen.

On Saturday we went to two museums and in the evening walked over to the entrance to the Arsenal, along the little canals leading to it were a lot of boats tied up waiting for the procession next day. It was wonderful to see them, they had elaborately carved prows, painted and gilded.

I had purposely chosen our holiday to include the Regatta which takes place on the first Sunday afternoon in September. In the morning we went to Mass at the church of San Moise where Ivan helped the resident priest with the service. It always looks to me as if the vestments the priests wear are made from old lace curtains. A very small congregation and we were only given a wafer, no wine which seems fairly normal in Catholic churches.

We then went round the Ducal Palace and I think it must have been then that we queued for about half an hour, it is often much longer, to go in to the Treasury of San Marco.

Lunched at Raffaels, and then went and looked for somewhere to watch the procession. It was not that easy to find a place on the Grand Canal, there were many people already lining the canal and also many places where it is not possible to get next to the water, finally sat on the steps of La Salute which was a good vantage point. There were two very long boats with about eighteen scullers in each. There were all the boats we had seen the night before with the gilding shining in the sunlight, the pageantry was indeed stunning. People in the boats were dressed in medieval costume; there were races of various kinds.

Before we left Venice we went to see the Scala Contarini del Bovolo which I had not seen before. Built in the 15th century, it is rather hidden away in the courtyard of Palazzo Contarini near Campo Mania and is an incredibly elegant spiral staircase that winds up a tower and was built by Giovanni Candi in marble and brick.

I still had two or three days in Rome and on one of these Ivan took me to a little shop Era Roma in the Via del Mascherino, which sold reproductions of ancient Roman things. I bought a little Medusa head pendant and a replica Etruscan baby's feeding bottle in the shape of a cockerel in pottery, called an Askos, there are some in the museum in Tarquinia and they date to the XI to the XIX century BC.

Appendix

Her memoirs end abruptly with a visit to Rome in 2002, her last trip abroad. It is not known whether she had intended to continue with her story or whether she would have included a number of handwritten musings that were found with her manuscript. A decision has been made to include the following as it is believed they supplement her story and enhance our knowledge of her and her activities.

Local Shopping

I did not have far to go for the shopping. We lived in Wellington Street and just round the corner was Cambray which leads into the High Street. Across the road was Dean's Wet Fish shop, all laid out on a slab. On the other side of the Co-op passageway was the Co-op butchery department where we bought meat. A step or two across the road was the Cadena where I bought two lbs of ground coffee a week (we were very much coffee drinkers). There was also a vegetable shop within a few steps, no need to drive out to a super market in those days.

Setting up the Flat over Elston Boutique

After my father died my mother moved to a more modern house at Hatherley. It was a twenty five minute walk to the shop so I spent quite a lot of time walking to and fro. When she started the shop, the first floor was only used for storage and I asked if I could live there. I quite enjoyed fitting it out and was allowed money from my father's estate to put in central heating. I painted the walls of the bathroom copying the Roman gardens of Livia. I made bookshelves, and fitted curtains to the three bay windows of the main room with thick Indian cotton in a darkish acid red. In the narrow kitchen I put the base of the Regency dresser from Wellington Street. In Regency times most terrace houses had pine dressers in the basements and this one was no less than six feet long, three deep drawers and above there were originally shelves for crockery.

The living room of my flat above the shop

Setting up the Coach House

It must have been about thirty years later as I approached sixty years old that I started to think of retirement. I began walking the streets looking for a suitable house in which to live plus room to set up a showroom which I would use one day a week, where my regular customers could continue to purchase their clothes if they wished. This way I could continue to earn a minor living. I decided on a coach house in Parabola Close, only a few minutes from the shop and I obtained permission to use part of it to trade.

The Coach House surrounded a central courtyard with my living quarters ahead and a wing on the right-hand side, which I would use as the showroom. My building firm that we had known for many years, moved in and worked intermittently on it all for about six months.
I found a pair of those large double doors that Regency houses often had between rooms on the ground or second floors and they were installed in the large room on the ground floor. I stripped them to the fairly pale colour of the pine - they led into the kitchen and I painted a design similar to early Chinese wallpaper on the walls each side. The staircase was of the ladder variety which I felt was rather too modern for the function I should use so the builders filled in the sides.

Living Room

Amina's office

Amina outside her home

Having grown to womanhood during World War II, I never expected to have everything new so furniture was composed of what was to hand or what I bought in second-hand shops. After she moved my mother had never used the set of Regency chairs from Wellington Street so I appropriated them and used them round a circular table that I found at 'old Charlie Fry's'. Anyone who lived in Cheltenham during the 1960's will remember old Charlie Fry's place. One would see a collection of old furniture and bits and pieces at the side of the road. There were two fields full of dilapidated chairs with black rabbits running about beneath them. This was old Charlie Fry's domain and I visited it often.

One could pick up a chair for a few shillings and once I remember going there with some friends and bringing back my mahogany round dining table on a pedestal base, and a good William IV swivel table. Three friends helped me to carry it to the new house.

[I also remember Fry's place as a confusing mass of old buildings, sheds etc. set in a large overgrown open area. The whole place was a maze of junk and, mostly Victorian, furniture of every description.

When Fry passed away there was an auction that attracted a large number of people, including myself. Ed.]

My grandparents had used a large Pembroke table they had bought when they married from an old man who had it from the Fleece Hotel in the lower High Street, where it had formed part of an enormous table used on market days from which farmers used to take their lunch. There are still brass connectors underneath where it was joined to the other similar parts of the table.

My parents had a three-piece suite and I saved one of armchairs and had it re-upholstered in the same fabric as a Regency settee that Olive Blackham had given me. I bought a nice card table from Dicks, who had a large shop full of second hand furniture opposite the Bowling Green in the lower High Street and later two Chinese style chairs from a place near Burford where they were made. Even here they seemed to give me a discount. I think they thought I was an interior designer.

Everything came together very easily, we had two War Department desks we had been using in the shop, these I stripped and painted part white. They went into my bedroom beside a wall made of louvre doors that had formed most of the fitting room in the shop.

In the bathroom I replaced the suite and unit, and then cut stencils of capitals and urns and painted the walls to represent a Roman room.

Marionettes

Later I made a marionette show of my own and gave performances at Cheltenham parties. I made a theatre out of laths of wood covered with blue and yellow felt. I stood on two large boxes to work the marionettes. It took me about two hours to erect & prepare and an hour to pack up after the show. The puppets varied a lot in size "Poppet", was I think the largest, he could be said to have 'run' the show and kept the children well entertained. In the other hand I worked a ------ (later a string a large heads?) and he would say 'up' and 'down' which words the --------- also short out. I did a number of fables (I remember carving the ----- head on my nineteenth birthday). There was the "Fox and the Crow", The "Lion and the Mouse" and "The Hare and the Tortoise". I did Edward Lear's "Pobble who lost his toes" and "The Dancing Horses".

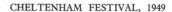

CHELTENHAM FESTIVAL, 1949

The Roel Puppets

Presented by Olive Blackham in association with Cheltenham Corporation

TOWN HALL, 3 and 5 p.m.

Wednesday - **29th June**

Friday - **1st July**

Saturday - **2nd July**
(Two Special Shows for Children of all ages)

Monday - **4th July**

Wednesday - **6th July**
(Apart from special performances on Saturday, the Shows are not suitable for Children under 10)

DIFFERENT PROGRAMMES at 3 and 5 p.m. each day (except Saturday)

Double sided leaflet

THE PROGRAMMES WILL INCLUDE :

A Chinese Folk Play

The Proposal by *Anton Tchehov*

Abraham and Isaac

The Courtship of the Yonghy-Bonghy-Bo

A Japanese Noh Play *translated by Ezra Pound*

etc., etc.

TICKETS - - 2/6
(reserved but not numbered)
On Saturday 2nd July, Children 1/6
Tickets from Town Hall   Telephone 2200

2071 Taylor, Young (Printers) Ltd., Cheltenham

The MG Midget

At one point my father started to teach me how to drive. Perhaps he expected me to be a natural but I was not. All I could think of was, this is a lethal weapon and I do not know what to do with it. I cannot remember how the matter ended or when I began to have classes with a professional but I passed my test at the second attempt by which time I had had 60 lessons. This always seems to surprise people that I took so long, but I never had any problems after that and drove with every confidence.

My Father had left a trust fund and after he had died, I was allowed to have sufficient money to buy a car. In 1969 I bought an MG Midget with wire wheels new for £800. It was really a very good investment as by time I had to stop driving 40 years later, because I could not see well enough, it was worth £7000. I had driven one and a half times round the clock and had very little trouble with it. It was serviced regularly with only two lots of major work on it [including one restoration], in all that time and only twice did it let me down, once when a fan belt broke and another when I ran out of petrol by mistake. Over the years I covered most of the British Isles, on one occasion I took it across the Channel to France, and I recall visiting various churches and cathedrals. It was always kept in a garage and our relationship was a very happy one. [Amina gave the MG to Richard Cornfield, a clergyman at Christchurch, her local church, who later displayed it as a classic car in the Edinburgh area. Ed.]

One of my first trips I made was to Hay-on-Wye to see the bookshops and stayed overnight in the ruins of Llanthony Priory, one could get bed and breakfast there. It was not an unmitigated success as I did not sleep well, I could hear a scrabbling in the walls which I thought might be rats. Next day driving over the pass was rather hazardous. It was a narrow road with a precipitous incline on one side. I think it was probably a bank holiday weekend so there was a great deal of traffic and I had to keep pulling off the road (the precipitous side of course!) to allow traffic to pass. It was quite a rite of passage.

My driving life was remarkably free of problems, one of the worst was when driving to Cardiff to examine A Level puppetry. A small piece of paper must have blown up from the floor of the car (I should have made sure there was nothing of value there when the roof was down, but presumably not on that day). It attracted my attention and I hit the curb for what seemed minutes but was probably only seconds. I struggled with the car before coming to rest on the grass verge facing in the opposite direction!

Amina
with her car

Gold Mine

I often went into Wales with David Bick and his friend George Hall, looking at mining sites, they both wrote books on Welsh mining. For several years I used to go to a course at Aberystwyth University with David Bick and Roy & Joan Day. We didn't do much attending the course but spent most of our days examining mining sites and sometimes going to the National Library of Wales to do research. I think it was there that I read about the Dolaucothi Mines.

The car gave me the opportunity to travel myself to places that interested me. One of them was Dolaucothi near Pumsaint, Carmarthenshire where the Romans, while they occupied Britain, mined for gold. Open cast working, trenching and adits extend over half a mile along the hillside to the southeast of the Cothi Valley. There is much to see there and although it must be forty years since I made my visit I clearly remember a good deal. I stayed the night at a bed and breakfast so I must have spent most of two days exploring the area. It is thought that the ancient workings exploited quartz reefs carrying free gold. A large mound of broken quartz the size of nuts is to be found in the fields below the mining area.

Near a cleared open space suitable for a car park, I found an entrance to a cave or workings. At Ogofao Lodge I saw a stone quern for grinding up stones and not far away stands Carreg Pumsaint, a boulder about two and a half feet high and worn into a number of hollows where quartz grinding must have taken place. In the woods I managed to find the coffin-shaped entrance of an adit, namely wider at the top then its bottom to allow a miner to carry a sack of stone across his shoulders. I walked through it until it opened out again in daylight.

There is a leat some seven miles long, running between the Cothi and Annell rivers. It led water from a narrow waterfall called 'Pwll Uffern which if my memory is correct is known as 'the Gate to Hell', down to a series of settling tanks above the workings. I made my way along the side of the river on a path, often no wider than a ledge, to the waterfall, it was altogether an impressive work.

G. W. Hall gives the history of later workings in "The Metal Mines of South Wales", 1971.

Jack Chalker

Memory plays strange tricks, today I was looking through a book that had arrived when I saw a colour plate of British prisoners of war with the Japanese during World War II, working in a cutting when they were building the Burmese Railway. There below the picture I saw a sketch of Konyu Hintok cutting, Thailand, by Jack Chalker, 1942. It was as if I had been punched between the eyes, memories came flooding back. It must have been not long after the war, but where did I meet him, how did I know him, had we met at the art school or where? Before the war he had been training at the Royal College of Art in London, when he was called up and becoming a prisoner of war worked on building the railway, that would run down the length of Burma, suffering the most incredible hardships. He survived and at some point became Art Master at the Cheltenham Ladies College. At first he must have been staying in one of the hotels because I remember him telling me that an old lady who used to sit in the lounge of one of them say "I can talk to anyone because my husband was a general"! He asked me if I would sit for him and we spent many pleasant hours in some small room at the College while he painted a portrait.

In 1950 he left Cheltenham for Falmouth, becoming Principal at the College of Art. Later he went to the College of Art in Bristol.

Cheltenham Festivals

For many years Cheltenham had musical festivals, even as far back as the years I was working with Olive Blackham, as I remember giving a marionette performance in a side room at one of them.

At first they were musical festivals and as time went on there were also literary and science festivals. Once I had entered my 80's and began to have trouble with my eyes it has been easier to watch TV than to read. I enjoyed hearing reports from around the world and liked to see the people who made them. Among the first I saw at a festival was Martin Bell, known as 'the man in the white suit' and Fergal Keane, these were followed by John Simpson and other well-known names. I remember sitting in a marquee behind the Town Hall with rain pouring on the flapping roof as we waited for Mark Urban to arrive; his train was late and the poor chap arrived wet and breathless to give his talk. I was especially glad to meet John Humphrys who read the news on the radio, I bought one of his books and he was very pleasant when he signed it. It all added to the interest of the heard and spoken word.

In later years it was always difficult to buy a ticket for Professor Brian Cox, as he was so popular. When I first saw him I marvelled at the way he seemed capable of smiling and talking at the same time. I found him a brilliant speaker and dishy in appearance and describing his subject in a very clear and understandable way, though a lack of knowledge of science on my part made it difficult for me to fully comprehend the planets and the universe.

Amina's Family

On looking back one can see that families are a small example of the way generations and the work they do changes. When my parents came together, a Marconi telegraph operator on board ship and my mother a dancer, their professions were new to the recent family. My father came from a family of successful industrialists in Birmingham. Thomas Chatwin, my great grandfather, had a factory in Great Tindal Street, manufacturing stocks, dies and taps, hand-power screwing machines, cylindrical gauges and drills. My Chatwin grandfather, Walter, was trained as an accountant, doubtless to work in the firm. In later years he lived on farms in Gloucestershire, presumably on money coming from the family firm.

On my mother's side my great grandfather, heavily bearded, was as a young man a journeyman boot maker, who walked from Devon to the Cheltenham area where he married. They had two sons and two daughters.

Pedigree of Amina Chatwin's Family
by the Editor

Chatwin Family

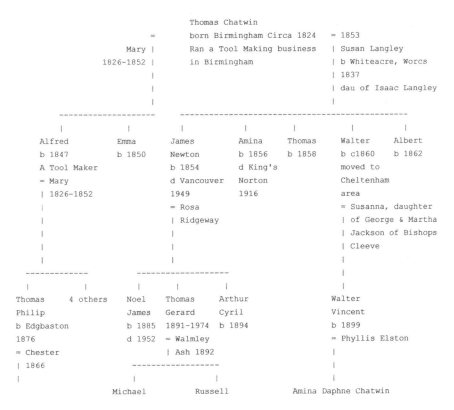

```
                                Thomas Chatwin
                    =           born Birmingham Circa 1824      = 1853
                Mary |          Ran a Tool Making business      | Susan Langley
                1826-1852 |     in Birmingham                   | b Whiteacre, Worcs
                          |                                     | 1837
                          |                                     | dau of Isaac Langley
                          |                                     |
        --------------------    ------------------------------------------------
        |           |           |           |           |           |           |
     Alfred      Emma        James       Amina       Thomas      Walter      Albert
     b 1847      b 1850      Newton      b 1856      b 1858      b c1860     b 1862
     A Tool Maker            b 1854      d King's                moved to
     = Mary                  d Vancouver Norton                  Cheltenham
     | 1826-1852             1949        1916                    area
     |                       = Rosa                              = Susanna, daughter
     |                       | Ridgeway                          | of George & Martha
     |                       |                                   | Jackson of Bishops
     |                       |                                   | Cleeve
     |                       |                                   |
     -------------           --------------------                |
     |          |            |          |            |           |
  Thomas    4 others      Noel      Thomas       Arthur       Walter
  Philip                  James     Gerard       Cyril        Vincent
  b Edgbaston             b 1885    1891-1974    b 1894       b 1899
  1876                    d 1952    = Walmley                 = Phyllis Elston
  = Chester                         | Ash 1892                |
  | 1866                            ------------------         |
  |                       |                      |            |
            Michael            Russell       Amina Daphne Chatwin
```

Pedigree of Amina Chatwin's Family
by the Editor

Elston Family

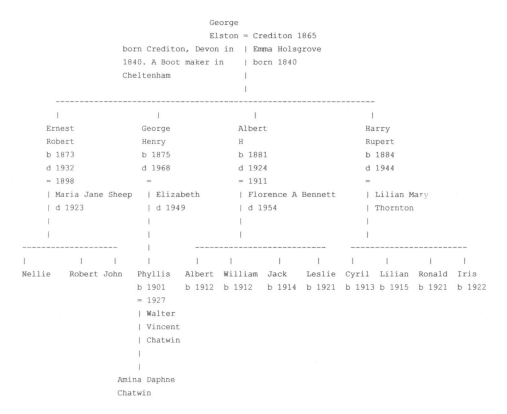

```
                        George
                        Elston = Crediton 1865
              born Crediton, Devon in | Emma Holsgrove
              1840. A Boot maker in   | born 1840
              Cheltenham              |
                                      |
       ------------------------------------------------------------------
       |                    |                    |                    |
     Ernest              George               Albert               Harry
     Robert              Henry                H                    Rupert
     b 1873              b 1875               b 1881               b 1884
     d 1932              d 1968               d 1924               d 1944
     = 1898              =                    = 1911               =
     | Maria Jane Sheep  | Elizabeth          | Florence A Bennett | Lilian Mary
     | d 1923            | d 1949             | d 1954             | Thornton
     |                   |                    |                    |
     |                   |                    |                    |
   ---------------------  |           -----------------------------  -------------------------
   |       |       |      |       |       |       |       |       |       |       |       |
 Nellie  Robert  John  Phyllis  Albert William  Jack   Leslie  Cyril  Lilian  Ronald  Iris
                       b 1901   b 1912 b 1912  b 1914  b 1921 b 1913 b 1915  b 1921 b 1922
                       = 1927
                       | Walter
                       | Vincent
                       | Chatwin
                       |
                       |
                     Amina Daphne
                     Chatwin
```

The JCB

There has been a JCB working within view of one of my windows. I have rather enjoyed watching it, one could almost see the machine thinking - if I push that over there and pile it up here. I'll be able to pick it up easier. After a bit I felt it was relevant to my own life.

I am a JCB
Clearing the rubbish.
Watch how I push it
And pile it, sorting it out.
Where should I put this?
Where should that go?
Once it was simple
But now it's too much
Too many books
And not enough shelves
Too many papers
Overflowing the files.
There was a time
When I knew
Where everything was
But now I spend
Half my life
Looking for things.
Eighty years of hoarding
Has left me overwhelmed.
I wish I knew the answer
Please tell me what to do -
A great big conflagration
And start everything anew?

[Some years ago Amina witnessed a development at the rear of a large house in Bayshill Road. Ed.]

171

In a Hospital Waiting Room

Sitting in a hospital waiting room waiting for an inspection into one of my eyes I had as good a laugh I have ever had in such a situation. A lady nearby was telling her friend of looking after a little boy while his mother was away having a baby. She asked him "would you rather have a little brother or a little sister?" to which the lad replied "If mum could manage it I'd rather have a pony"!!!

Obituary to Amina by Julian Rawes

Amina was a unique and interesting character and I do hope that this eulogy does her justice. She was kind, gentle and caring but many were the times that we, like many others, came under her hammer. One instance comes to mind when Joy and I took her out to lunch to the National Trust pub at Bretforton. While we were perusing the menu a presentable young man approached and asked us what we wanted to drink, which is what tends to happen nowadays. That was the cue for Amina to say in a way that only she could "Why do people ask what one wants to drink before one has chosen the food?" The room went quiet, the poor waiter looked shocked, we cringed and I later apologised to the waiter. Now Amina was technically correct, after all she had been cook/housekeeper to the British Military Attaché in Paris, in a time and place when etiquette was all important. Well, that was Amina and I for one loved her all the same, she was a lovely lady.

In fact I can hear her now above me saying NO NO that's not the way to say it.

Amina Chatwin was a real Cheltonian of the old school and acted as such. She was born in the family home, a Regency house in Wellington Street, in 1927. She was an only child and was educated in a small private school nearby.

In her memoirs her adventures that were to encapsulate her life started early. "When I was baby I was for a time looked after by a Nurse Stenhouse. She must have been a rather odd character because one day she decided that she must go to London. With admirable care for her charge, and having no one to leave me with, she set off to walk to London pushing me in my pram. She wrote a note to my parents, which was not discovered until late afternoon, probably when my father returned from work. At all events he set off in his car to find us and caught up with us at Northleach, so we had travelled quite a distance. I do not think that she remained long in our employ after this episode."

She appears to have had a happy childhood and was introduced to a number of activities by her parents, such as dancing and learning to ride. She would often visit her grandparents who made beautiful civil and military riding boots in a shop in Winchcombe Street. Her grandmother was a dressmaker, a skill that was inherited by both Amena and her mother. It was because of this tradesman connection that she was apparently refused entry to Cheltenham Ladies Collage - Cheltenham of a past age!

In 1935, when the open-air swimming pool was opened she was chosen as a child model and wore a bathing costume and carried a bucket and spade and towelling cloak, accompanying three lady models.

Her father was interested in fossils and would take her with him and she learnt that the Cotswolds were once under the sea. She also loved books and history books in particular. Her school was keen on Shakespeare and visits to the Opera House were frequent. All this clearly sparked later interests.

She had memories of WW2 and its effect on Cheltenham. One event was seeing Amy Johnson drive into the Plough Hotel courtyard. She also learnt to fire her father's sporting gun.

Amina was obviously good at English from an early age. Her mother was keenly interested in dancing and ran a dancing school for most of her life and it was probably due to this that Amina qualified as a Licentiate of the Guildhall School of Music and Drama so that she could introduce Speech training at her mother's school. She trained at ballet but did not continue with it, preferring the ballroom, which was to figure strongly and she was clearly good at it becoming, with her partner Ron, both Gloucestershire and West of England champions. This hobby enabled her to travel far and wide being on one occasion at the Royal Albert Hall. She had started making puppets during the war and as time went on began to work with Olive Blackham as an assistant, an extraordinary woman who had developed marionettes for adult shows. Olive lived in Wellington Street and long and the short of it was that she and Amina toured the country with their puppet shows and puppetry exhibitions. Olive's puppets were often some two-and-a-half to three foot high and could be very heavy to operate. Her dear friend died in 2002 aged 103. In the 1950's she attended art school and has painted some very nice paintings. At this time she started her travels to the continent, on the earlier occasions on the back of a motor bike. She was always attracted by the historical and architectural scenery.

In 1957 she took a different course and answered an advert in The Lady to become the cook/housekeeper for the British Military Attaché in Paris, his wife and children and through that job, travelled extensively. She studied at the Cité Universitaire, met all sorts of people and travelled to North Africa. This opened up a huge new world to Amina and it is clear that she enjoyed all these experiences immensely.

In 1960 she joined a Workers Educational Association study holiday looking at Prehistoric cave paintings in the Pyrenees. It was a fateful trip as it was here that she met my father and, remarkably three other people who became her life-long friends, Ivan Page, Derek Jackson and Cedric Neilsen.

Her first printed work appeared in 1961, not on history or ironwork, but ballet with a discourse on its changing styles. It was in the 1960's that she started to join a number of societies and we come to the world of Amina that we know. She joined the Gloucestershire Society for Industrial Archaeology, formed in 1963, of which she became its secretary, editor and eventually president; the Bristol and Gloucestershire Archaeological Society, GADARG and others. She wrote a number of papers, and published her book on Cheltenham's ironwork and distributed it herself. She was seen frequently on society trips and at meetings, staged many dinner parties and slide shows.

After her father died she bought a new white MG midget for £800 and drove it until about ten years ago when it was worth £7000. After his death she got more involved with her mother and her dancing school come dress shop called Elstone Studios near the Rotunda. Amina took on the dress making side of things and eventually took over the business calling it Elstone Boutique, which she ran for 30 years. She lived above the shop until her mother died when she sold it and bought her present abode.

In 1963 she joined the newly set up Historical Metallurgy Society and produced its newsletter from 1985 to 2003. She visited the USA twice, travelling with groups from the British Artists Blacksmiths Association and later took part in a 2000 mile journey through Europe with a group of 32 American blacksmiths on a tour organised by the Artist Blacksmith Association of North America.

She also took a strong interest in Cheltenham society and history, was a member of Cheltenham Local History Society from its inception and an active supporter of the art gallery and museum.

She left two unpublished manuscripts that I will ensure are published. One is a major history of ironworking from the earliest times the other is her autobiography.

Amina was a highly sociable and intelligent person who was interested in and had opinions on everything. It is only now that I have learned of the large number of charities she supported ranging from the British Legion, Salvation Army, Red Cross to the Donkey Sanctuary at Sidmouth, Dorset. Strong, snappy but a gentle and caring person who gave much to society. She will be remembered with kindness and affection.

[A fine obituary to Amina Chatwin was published by Dick Quinnell in the journal of the British Artist Blacksmiths Association (BABA).]

Amina hosting a Christmas dinner

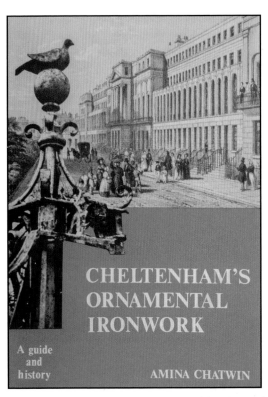

*Cheltenham's Ornamental
Ironwork*

*A Guide and History
1974*

*by
Amina Chatwin*

ISBN: 0 9503820 0 0

INTO THE NEW IRON AGE

*Modern British Blacksmiths
1995*

*by
Amina Chatwin*

ISBN: 0 9525105 0 2

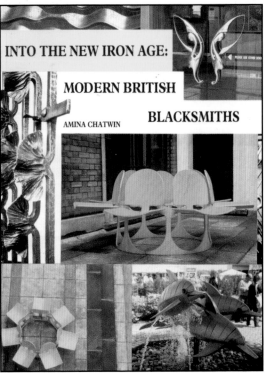